Everyday Life Lessons
Living Life with Ease and Grace

Companion Guide

Patricia Zimmerman

WDC PUBLISHING CO., INC.
Light always overcomes the darkness

Everyday Life Lessons: Living Life with Ease and Grace — Companion Guide
Copyright © 2018 Patricia M. Zimmerman. All rights reserved.

No part of this book may be used or reproduced in any manner whatsoever without prior written permission of the publisher except for "fair use" as brief quotations embodied in critical articles and reviews. Requests for permission or further information should be addressed to WDC Publishing Co. Inc.

The author of this book does not dispense medical advice or advocate the use of any technique as a form of treatment either directly or indirectly for physical, psychological, or medical problems without the advice of a physician. The intent of the author is only to offer information of a general nature to help you in your quest for emotional and spiritual well-being. In the event you use any of the information in this book for yourself, which is your constitutional right, the author and the publisher assume no responsibility for your actions.

Published and distributed in the United States by WDC Publishing. For information, contact WDC Publishing Co., Inc. at info.wdcpublishing@gmail.com.

Cover design by Mary Beth Wilker, Wilker Design and Marketing
Consultant: Steven Bauer, Hollow Tree Literary Services
ISBN: 978-0-9962475-6-6

Library of Congress Cataloging-in-Publication Data: Not available at time of printing.

Dedication

This book is dedicated to all those who struggle to find meaning and purpose in life.

We are here to heal, not to harm.
We are here to love, not to hate.
We are here to create, not to destroy.
We are ALL One.
~ Anonymous

Always pray to have
eyes that see the best in people,
a heart that forgives the worst,
a mind that forgets the bad,
and a soul that never loses faith in God.
~ Anonymous

Acknowledgements

My sincerest and deepest gratitude to all those who have loved and supported me on my journey, for without you this book would not have been possible:
- To Source/God and all of the Divine, to whom I dedicate my life and all that I do.
- To my mother, Barbara Markowski, and my husband, Chuck — for your unending love and support, for your faith in me, and for your acceptance of my journey.
- To my children, their spouses, and my grandchildren — for your patience with me as I walk this path. It is not an easy path to walk, but it is truly a most rewarding one!
- To Elliott and Diane Jackson — My life changed when we met, and I will be forever grateful for all you have done and will do for me and for White Dove Circle of Light and Love.
- To my many teachers in Spirit and in the physical — thank you for helping me on my journey. You helped me to remember who I Am and that life

PATRICIA ZIMMERMAN

does not have to be as difficult or as miserable as we choose to make it.

I love you all so very much! Namaste.

Synopsis

There is a spiritual awakening taking place, and the momentum is building. Can you feel it? People are beginning to wake up, realizing there is more to life than what we have been taught. People are eager to understand life and how it really works. They want to know why mankind suffers and what it will take to change the world. They are searching for answers, and they want Truth.

Life is simple, yet we make it complicated. When you open your mind to expand your knowledge, you begin to look at life from a different perspective—one that makes perfect sense!

Everyday Life Lessons: Living Life with Ease and Grace was written for those who struggle to find meaning and purpose in life. Earth is a school that teaches many lessons. The goal of any student is to graduate. This book will help you to graduate from this school called Earth.

This book will help you better understand the gift of free choice and our journey back to Oneness with God. It explains how you planned your life before coming into physical form and how you create your life with every choice you make. It details a map for success and teaches how to attain and maintain prosperity. It contains tools for health and well-being, for protection, and for spiritual growth.

Life is a gift. Embrace life and all it has to offer.

About the Author

Patricia M. Zimmerman is an ordained minister, spiritual counselor, metaphysical teacher, healing practitioner, author, and founder of White Dove Circle of Light and Love, a spiritual, non-profit organization where one can find true healing for the mind, body, and spirit. She teaches classes on how to live life, looking at the self to bring about change. Her greatest teacher is life itself.

This is her second book. Her first, *Self-Empowerment: The Only Way to Live*, came out in 2015.

Table of Contents

Tools for Health and Well-Being   1
  Acid vs. Alkaline
  Breathe!
  Crystals
  Crystal Remedies
  Dealing with Anxiety and Depression
  Eating Organic
  Essential Oils
  Herbal Remedies / Teas
  Grounding
  Journaling
  Kinesiology
  Muscle Testing
  Raising Self-Esteem
  Relationships
  Releasing Stress
  Self-Healing Techniques
  Setting Personal Boundaries
  Taking Time for You
  The Attitude of Gratitude

The Importance of a Good Cleanse
The Importance of a Well-Balanced Diet
The Importance of Nutrition
The Proper Amount of Hydration

Tools for Clearing and Protection   47
Cutting Cords of Attachment
Help with Challenging People and Situations
Releasing Low Vibration Entities
Space Clearing
The Platinum Shield

Tools for Spiritual Growth   63
Beauty Raises Vibration
Codes of Conduct for a Disciple of the Holy Spirit
Decrees
Faith
Ho'Oponopono
How to Recognize True Messengers
Listening to Your Inner Guidance
Manifestation
Prayer and Meditation
Raising Your Vibration
Relationships
Release Letters
Trust and Surrender

Disclaimer

What I share with you in this book are my truths. If they resonate with you, they will become your truths, too. My truths were learned from the hundreds of spiritual books I've read over a span of thirty-plus years on my quest for Truth. My truths also come from my experiences in life, my experience in past-life regression, and my experience in helping others to heal their lives. Experience is the best teacher there is.

Always keep an open mind. People who refuse to open their minds to the truth are not ready to hear it. Life is fair when you open your mind to Truth. As John Heywood once stated in 1546, "There is none so blind as those who will not see." The most misguided people in the world are those who choose to keep a closed mind.

Truth is Truth. God's Truth never changes and needs no defending. If one must build an army to defend one's truth, then one is not working with God's Truth (Absolute Truth). If hearing the Truth angers one, that person's perception of truth is not Truth.

Our soul always recognizes that which is Truth. The spirit must seek it. The Truth shall set you free!

Introduction

"Remember, when you are making upward spiritual progress, lower portions of the universe will make attempts to bring you down."
~ Source/God through Elliott Eli Jackson

Life is fair when we understand how it works. Life does not have to be difficult. We make it difficult when we listen to the ego (Edging God Out) instead of our inner guidance, and what we resist persists.

Life is a process. We hear people say: "Two steps forward, one step backward." Rushing the process never works. If we skip a step along the way, we will go back to learn it. Do not try to force life. Everything takes place in Divine Timing, and Divine Timing is always perfect!

To bake a cake, one must have all the ingredients. If you leave one of the ingredients out, the cake will fail. When the batter is ready, it is put into pans to bake in the oven. If pulled out too soon, the cake falls. If left in too long, it burns. Having all of the ingredients and perfect timing are crucial for a successful outcome.

The body is a finely-tuned instrument. When one body is out of alignment, they are all out of alignment. When we take unnecessary supplements and medication, we throw off the chemistry of the physical body. For example, too much or too little oil in a car or fluid in the transmission can break a car down. Putting water in the gas tank will do the same.

If we love ourselves, every day we will:
- take time for prayer (talk to God)
- meditate (10 minutes every day)
- eat healthy (eat organic whenever possible)
- take the necessary vitamins and supplements (muscle test to know what your body needs and the correct dosage)
- exercise (15-30 minutes, 2-3 times a week, depending on your ability)

If we do not love ourselves enough to take time for us, no one else will. Synchronicity takes place when all our bodies are in sync and our vibration is high. And when we are in alignment, magic, mystery, and miracles take place!

We can live a life with ease and grace...and learn our lessons at the same time. It's all in how we handle life. Everything happens for a reason and a purpose. This book came to you because you were ready for change. By changing your beliefs and your attitude, the world around you will change, too—*for the better!*

EVERYDAY LIFE LESSONS: LIVING LIFE WITH EASE AND GRACE

The following tools can help you to live a life with ease and grace. And, as I remind all my students often, ***tools are no good if you don't use them!*** Blessings to you on your journey!

Tools for Health and Healing

"Health does not always come in the form of medicine. Most of it comes from peace of mind, peace in the heart, peace of soul. It comes from laughter and love." ~ Anonymous

Acid vs. Alkaline

Cancer cells cannot grow and disease cannot exist in a high alkaline body. The body stays strong when pH is maintained. Spiritually thinking, alkaline is symbolic of love and acid is symbolic of fear.

Normal pH is 7.0–7.4. The ideal pH level is 7.4 or higher so all the functions of the body perform effortlessly. Test strips (available at most pharmacies), also known as litmus paper, provide an inexpensive way to monitor pH levels. To use the test strips, place a small amount of saliva or urine on the strip and wait for the color to change. Compare the pH color on the strip with the pH color on the box to find your pH number.

If your body's pH is low, you are probably low on minerals such as sodium, potassium, magnesium, and calcium.[1]

A diet of 80 percent alkaline- and 20 percent acid-forming foods is recommended to maintain proper balance.

Breathe!

For a more joyous outlook on life and to calm the emotions, take time to breathe. Breathe in the breath of God using deep breaths at least twice a day.

Empty the lungs of stale breath. Form the mouth into an "oo" sound and breathe out heavily. Stand erect, with your feet together and your arms resting at your sides.

- Slowly inhale (filling the diaphragm) to the count of five, raising your arms over your head. As you inhale, push the diaphragm out.
- Hold to the count of five while visualizing a shaft of Golden White Light pouring down from your crown chakra and going through every part of your body and into your energy field.
- Exhale to the count of five, slowly lowering the arms back down to the sides.
- Hold to the count of five.

Repeat this seven times. This is a great way to release stress and bring you back into balance.

Crystals

About Crystals

Crystals have been used to assist in the healing process for thousands of years. They have been mentioned in the Bible. The high priest Aaron used them in his breastplate to communicate with angels. King Solomon's ring (gemstone) gave him power over the elements.

Throughout history, precious and semi-precious stones (crystals) were used in the crowns of kings and queens and in the statues of gods and goddesses, symbolizing their association with mystical powers. The diamond is used in wedding bands today as a symbol of purity.

Crystals are energy transmitters. They can absorb, focus, and transmit subtle electromagnetic energy; for example, watches and radios use quartz crystals. For this reason, they make excellent healing tools. Because crystals have a pure energy that vibrates at a fixed, stable, and unchangeable frequency, they can bring our energy level to their energy level. Upon coming into contact with a crystal, the vibrations of the crystal will interact with and change your vibration, bringing you back into a state of peace and harmony.

Crystals are used today in clocks, radios, microwaves, computers, and much more. There was resurgence in the use of crystals in the 1980s and 1990s. Interest in crystals grew and made headlines in newspapers, magazines, and television shows.

The human body cannot exist without minerals. Minerals can grow into crystals if they have enough space. Quite often there are so many different crystals growing in the same little space that none of the crystals are able to grow very large. The physical body can receive minerals from the crystal by placing the crystal on the body.

Resonance is the key principal of crystal healing. Since most matter is crystalline in nature, our bodies take on the energy being transmitted from the crystal. Quartz crystals have a similar molecular structure to water, which responds when charged with crystal energy by developing a more coherent crystalline structure. Since our bodies are mostly water, healing intentions directed and amplified through crystals can easily transfer to our bodies and stabilize our health.

Crystals can be used in many ways: for healing, meditation, protection, and manifestation, to name a few. They can be used as an elixir and to improve the health of plants and an aura.

Now that you know the basic principles behind charging crystals, their creative uses are limited only by your imagination and clarity of intent.

Crystal Basics

Place crystals under your bed to help you remember your dreams or to facilitate restful sleep (especially amethyst), over doorways and windows for protection, in the office for efficiency and productivity. They can also be carried in pockets or purses.

To open the heart, carry a rose quartz. To heal a broken heart, carry a black tourmaline to remove negative energy.

Clear quartz is an amplifier. It is the most popular crystal because its many geometric configurations can be used for many different purposes.

Amethyst is considered a powerful yet gentle master healer to transmute negative energy and facilitate cooperation, protection, and balance during times of transition.

Fluorite and pyrite stabilize the thinking process and can help with studying or doing mental work over long periods of time. Students should carry this stone with them during test time and also wear something yellow to easily connect with knowledge.

Wear a black tourmaline to ward off negativity. Morganite and kunzite help to absorb negativity.

Other popular crystals that help to reduce stress include citrine, hematite, malachite, smoky quartz, and turquoise.

Drink plenty of water after a healing session to flush out the toxins.

To learn more about crystals, my favorite authors

include: Katrina Raphaell, Melody, Judy Hall, Ken Harsch, Naisha Ahsian and Robert Simmons.

Cleansing Crystals

There are many ways to clear crystals. One way is by washing them with fresh (river, stream, or waterfall) or tap water to remove negative ions. A soft toothbrush can be used to clean crystal clusters. Crystals with a hardness of 4 or higher or made of salt (selenite, for example) should never set in water or they will dissolve. When in doubt, do not use water.

Set them in a bowl or pan of water with some Epsom or sea salt. Leave them there for 1-3 hours. Rinse them off.

Sound therapy can be used to clear crystals; e.g., crystal singing bowls, tuning forks, and Tibetan bells. The sound emitted must be of a higher frequency than the stone you are trying to cleanse.

Smudge crystals using cedar, bury them in the earth for 1-3 weeks, or bury them in sea salt to release negative ions. Do not use salt with porous, water- or metal-based crystals such as opal, lapis lazuli, malachite, or hematite. When in doubt, do not use salt.

Reiki energy can also be used to clear and charge crystals.

Some crystals, like citrine and kyanite, never need clearing.

Charging Crystals

Crystals are like batteries. The more you use them, the more their energy is depleted.

There are many ways to charge or re-energize crystals. Use nature by placing them outside in a safe place. Use sunlight to break down the negative ions and to re-energize them. To charge crystals for meditation or dream work, place them in moonlight.

Some crystals fade in sunlight, such as amethyst, kunzite. Never let them sit in sunlight for more than one-half hour at a time.

Place smaller crystals in a large cluster of crystals, such as quartz or amethyst, to cleanse and charge them.

Gridding with Crystals

The following are notes from a workshop taken years ago with Naisha Ahsian, co-author of the book, *The Book of Stones, Who They Are and What They Teach*:

A grid is a geometric form created from stones that have the geometry of the overall geometric form; e.g., quartz is hexagonal (6-sided) in its structure. An array is the way in which the crystals are laid out. Clear quartz and candle quartz work best to grid a room.

When creating a grid, use stones that have the same geometric form of the overall grid you plan to create. This creates a coherency because the overall form mimics the actual geometric sacred geometry of the crystal itself, creating a more cohesive energy within the grid itself. For example, use six 6-sided stones when creating a hexagon-shaped grid. The termination of the stone is considered the seventh point. When you sit in the center of that grid, you become the seventh point, the termination of the crystal grid. When tested with an electromagnetic meter, a discernably different frequency was noticed inside the grid than outside of the grid (as with crop circles).

Arrays are not constructed according to the geometrical structure of the stones; however, if you put an array inside a grid, the energy of the grid will be amplified. Arrays can be any combination of stones set in any formation. They can be used to bring in love and abundance, a deeper meditation experience, and more; however, there is no coherence in arrays because there are varying geometries, minerals, etc. going on within the set of stones. A grid will create the large coherent field, which will then amplify the energetic structure of the array placed within it.

The six stones in the grid must be activated to be resonant with each other. Sit with the stones and activate them through your heart, expanding your energy field (raising the volume) to incorporate all of the stones in the primary grid. Make sure all of the stones are activated so they work together. Activation is critical.

Once the stones are activated, the grid will remain

coherent until a "louder" energy comes along. Everything that comes into the grid will be amplified by it. Do not build a grid around your computer or you will amplify the microwaves coming off of your computer instead of mitigating them. This is why you should not use quartz around your computer. Quartz crystals are amplifiers. They easily resonate with microwave radiation and will amplify that microwave radiation. Do not use magnets around your computer or you can wipe it clean.

When gridding a room, size does matter. Use a larger crystal (approximately 6 inches in length) for a larger room and smaller crystals for a smaller room. Try to keep them all roughly the same size. They do not need to be huge. If your stones are too large, they cannot resonate with the intention for the grid because large stones have a large inherent amplitude, so it will take longer to achieve your goal.

Intention is important. Your frequency needs to be loud enough to shift the stones to bring in your desired intention.

The direction of the stone does make a difference. A clockwise crystal grid will create a vortex of energy. Clockwise vortexes are electrical vortexes that send energy out into the atmosphere. Counterclockwise vortexes are magnetic vortexes that draw energy in from outside the grid to the center of the grid.

To send a prayer out into the world, create a clockwise or electrical vortex. To bring in something you would like to manifest (e.g., prosperity, love), create a counterclockwise or magnetic vortex.

To bring in healing, create an etheric grid by standing your stones with the termination pointing up. Set the crystals in little flower pots with sand (¾ full). Sand is quartz and therefore an amplifier. The crystals create a forcefield as opposed to a vortex.

Crystals pointing toward the center of the grid are similar to a magnetic vortex because you bring energy in from the outside and focus it toward the middle. Crystals pointing outward from the grid are similar to an electrical vortex because your intention is sent outward into the world.

To protect a building, property, or garden, use 6-inch lengths of ¾-inch copper tubing. Cut the top of the tubing with a hacksaw so there are four petals on one end of the pipe. Set your crystal upright inside the copper tubing. Copper is an amplifier. Create the hexagon grid by digging six holes around the perimeter of the building, property, or garden. Place the quartz in copper tubing in the ground. Cover with dirt it so it is buried.

A neutral vortex is important when gridding a house. An electrical vortex in a house will make it difficult to stay grounded. A magnetic vortex can make you feel depressed; it will be difficult to raise a vibration. A neutral vortex will create a forcefield around the space to mitigate any external energies coming in.

Cloudy stones are just as effective as clear stones. For healing purposes, a single- or double-terminated quartz point will work. The internal structure of the stone, not its appearance, makes a difference in the outcome. Double-terminated quartz crystals do not work well for creating vortexes. To create a vortex, single-terminated quartz crystals work better because the energy goes in one direction only.

The color of a stone can be an indicator of the mineral concentration within the stone. For instance, a deep purple amethyst has more iron and magnesium, which can enhance a healing session. Even though the color in stones like amethyst and kunzite can be bleached out by the sun, the minerals are still there.

A crystal within 4 feet of your body will create a resonant field that can go wherever needed. Crystals do not have to touch the skin. All stones have energy, and they all work. River rocks and stones from the earth are more powerful stones.

Place crystals under your healing table to create a grid for healing, but keep in mind the resonance will not be high enough to encompass the client. It is better to grid the overall room so whatever you have under your table is amplified by the grid to ensure a positive outcome.

Animals are more sensitive to electromagnetic fields, which is why they can sense changes within the earth. Some crystals have too much energy for them. Be aware of this when working with animals.

All crystals are minerals, but not all minerals are crystals. Rocks are usually a balance of several different minerals. For example, granite has quartz, danburite, and other minerals. Crystals usually have one or two different minerals, while rocks may have more.

Simon and Shuster's *Guide to Rocks and Minerals* details the geometrical form, mineral content, etc. of a stone.

Healing with Crystals

Crystal healing works because of the principle of resonance. Most matter is crystalline in nature and will take on the energy transmitted via other crystals, such as quartz. Quartz crystals also have a similar molecular structure to water, which respond when charged with crystal energy by developing a more coherent crystalline structure. Since our bodies are mostly water, healing intentions directed and amplified through crystals can easily transfer to our bodies and stabilize our health.

Crystal Surgery is an intuitive art. Healing practitioners have become adept at using crystals like energetic scalpels to remove unwanted blocks and excess energy (as in migraines, fevers, headaches), or as energizers to add energy where needed. Healing takes place on the etheric body and automatically flows in the physical body. Crystal surgery is one of the very powerful healing methods used at White Dove Circle of Light and Love.

Crystal Remedies

Following are a few of the many healing remedies using crystals. Be sure to rinse the stones to clear and charge them when you are through with them.

For Protection from Negative Energy

Place a black tourmaline in your left pocket to ward off negative energy, and a rose quartz in your right pocket to send love. (We bring in with our left, and send out with our right.)

To Dispel Depression

Place a rose quartz in your left pocket to bring in love, and a black tourmaline in your right pocket to release negative thoughts and emotions.

To Drain the Sinuses

The sinuses are where we store the minor irritations in life, which is why so many people have sinus issues. We have 18-24 hours to release a negative emotion or we store it in the body.

To release these minor irritations, strategically place three citrine crystals on the head while lying down: one on the third eye (middle of the forehead, just above the eyebrows), one under the left eye on the cheek bone, and one under the right eye on the cheek bone. Close your eyes. Leave the stones in place for 10 minutes.

To Release a Headache or Migraine
Headaches and migraines signify the brain (our computer) is getting ready to shut down, usually the result of being stressed out or overthinking. Lie down and place a lepidolite in mica on the third eye. Leave it there for at least 30 minutes to clear and balance any negative or excess energy.

To Keep from Falling and to Release Vertigo
Vertigo and falling often are the result of unbalanced energy. Two similar-sized shiva linghams can help bring about balance by placing one stone in a pocket on one side of the body and the other stone in a pocket on the other side of your body. Carry them with you daily.

To Release Blockages, Swelling, Pain, etc.
Two stones that can release blockages, swelling, pain, etc., are a fluorite point and a Faden crystal. A fluorite point is a fluorite crystal with a shape similar to a quartz crystal. Its

termination consists of six triangles coming to a point at the top. A Faden crystal has a milky white, tube-like line of growth running from edge to edge through a quartz crystal. It can also be the blue vein running through a kyanite crystal.

Place the fluorite point (termination pointing up) or Faden crystal over the afflicted area. Hold it there for three to five minutes. The pulsing sensation felt is the stone releasing. Visualize a platinum shield at the end of the termination to transmute the negative energy into positive energy.

If using a fluorite point, take the terminated end of the fluorite point and basket weave the energy of the stone into your energy field when you are through releasing. Fluorite has healing properties. The energy from the stone will help to heal the afflicted area more quickly.

To Bring in Prosperity
Carry a small citrine stone in your wallet or purse.

Dealing with Anxiety and Depression

How to prevent an anxiety attack:
Breathe deeply three to four times, in through your nose and out through your mouth.

Use the five senses of sight, hearing, touch, smell, and

taste to help bring someone back to the present moment. Look around to find:
- 5 things you can see
- 4 things you can hear
- 3 things you can touch
- 2 things you can smell
- 1 thing you can taste

This type of grounding can help when you feel like you've gone too far in your head and lost control of your surroundings.

Thump the thymus to help center, focus, and balance.

To Dispel Depression

Anxiety and depression are also the result of low-vibration entities. Clear the lower vibrations from your energy field and spirit body daily by reciting a mantra to release them. Protect yourself daily by reciting the Platinum Shield. *(See Tools for Protection: Releasing Low-Vibration Entities and The Platinum Shield)*

Recite the twenty I Am Decrees given to us from Source/God through Elliott Eli Jackson to help raise your vibration and to help you to remember who you really are. Saying them daily will help to become a better you. *(See Tools for Spiritual Growth: Decrees.)*

Smudge your house. *(See Tools for Protection, Space Clearing)* Decorate with fresh eucalyptus. Low-vibration entities do not like eucalyptus! Diffuse eucalyptus or release essential oil (Young Living). Place a drop of eucalyptus oil on your crown chakra, your third eye, your throat chakra, your wrists, and the top of your feet to push away the low vibrations.

Refrain from drinking alcohol or using recreational drugs. This is so important because they attract lower vibrations. When you feel yourself becoming lightheaded ("getting high"), your spirit is going out and a low-vibration entity is coming in.

Never give your power away to anyone or anything!

Our diet is also a major contributing factor to the way we feel. Seven foods that could boost your serotonin: eggs, cheese, pineapples, tofu, salmon, nuts, and turkey.[2] Eat foods that ward off depression:[3]

- **Sweet potatoes:** rich in Vitamin B6. Low levels of B6 have been associated with symptoms of depression.
- **Spinach:** rich in tryptophan and folate. Tryptophan and folate increase serotonin levels in the brain. Serotonin is a neurotransmitter that helps us feel happy.
- **Cashews:** very rich in tryptophan. Eating two handfuls of cashews is the equivalent of one dose of Prozac.
- **Berries:** rich in polyphenols, an

anti-inflammatory. Inflammation (unshed tears) has been linked to symptoms of depression.
- **Avocados:** this superfood is rich in tryptophan, folate, and omega-3. Omega-3 has been known to reduce inflammation in the body and regulates the brain's neurotransmitters.

Bananas, almonds, apples, watermelons, cherries, yogurt, beans, eggs, and meats also increase dopamine levels in the body. Decrease sugar and caffeine intake. Avoid processed foods and junk food, which can lower the amount of magnesium in your body. Eat mangoes, which are high in magnesium, to calm the nerves. Take a daily vitamin and a high dose of a quality magnesium supplement, if necessary. Get plenty of exercise and the proper amount of sleep. Decrease stress. Set a routine schedule allowing for plenty of time for work and relaxation.[4]

Drink herbal teas. Eat high-alkaline foods. Dis-ease cannot settle into a body that is 7.8 or higher in alkaline. Alkaline represents love; acid represents fear.

Spend three to five minutes giving gratitude to God to totally shift your way of thinking and being. Gratitude will lift your spirit, raise your vibration, and help you to see the many blessings of life.

Be in service to others. When we are in service to others, we are too busy to feel depressed. It raises our vibration, pushing low-vibration entities away.

EVERYDAY LIFE LESSONS: LIVING LIFE WITH EASE AND GRACE

Meditation, not medication! Meditate at least 10 minutes every day to keep the blues away and to find peace within. When there is chaos in your life, there is chaos within. When there is peace within, there is peace in your life.

Play uplifting music, Native American flute, or classical music. This high-vibrational music raises your vibration and the vibration of the room.

Find joy in life by choosing to make time for you. Take time to be in nature. There's beauty in nature. It will help to ground you. Surround yourself with beauty. Find the beauty in life and in you.

Use and/or diffuse Frankincense essential oil, a proven antidepressant with no side effects, to help dispel depression. Use and/or diffuse uplifting therapeutic essential oils blended to raise your vibration. Modern Essentials guidebook recommends lavender, orange and lemon, or a grounding blend to dispel anxiety and lemon and frankincense to dispel depression.[5]

Place a rose quartz crystal in your left pocket to bring in love, and a black tourmaline in your right pocket to release negative thoughts and emotions. Wear a blue lace agate to help maintain a peaceful state of being.

Take a hot bath using a handful of Dead Sea salts and a few essentials oils; e.g., eucalyptus, lavender, rose, geranium, or jasmine.

Use all of these recommendations to make a powerful

antidote to keep the blues away with no side effects except happiness and well-being.

Eating Organic

The USDA National Organic Program (NOP) defines organic as: "food produced by farmers who emphasize the use of renewable resources and the conservation of soil and water to enhance environmental quality for future generations. Organic meat, poultry, eggs, and dairy products come from animals that are given no antibiotics or growth hormones. Organic food is produced without using most conventional pesticides; fertilizers made with synthetic ingredients or sewage sludge; or ionizing radiation. Before a product can be labeled 'organic,' a government-approved certifier inspects the farm where the food is grown to make sure the farmer is following all the rules necessary to meet USDA organic standards. Companies that handle or process organic food before it gets to your local supermarket or restaurant must be certified, too."[6]

A truly organic product will have a "100% Organic" logo on the packaging. "Organic" means the product is 95-99 percent organic, and "Made with Organic Ingredients" means the product is 70-94 percent organic.

According to an April 2012 AARP bulletin, to be able to tell if grocery store produce is truly organic, look at the Price Look Up (PLU) sticker. If the produce is organic, the code will contain five digits beginning with 9 (95023). Non-organic produce will only contain four digits (5023). A five-digit PLU beginning with 8 means the item is genetically modified (85023).[7]

When a product is labeled "Natural," harmful toxins may be used as ingredients. While the best place to get fresh produce is at a local farmer's market, it does not guarantee the produce was grown in an organic environment.

Essential Oils

Essential oils were one of the first medicines used by man. Egyptian and Chinese manuscripts show they have been used for thousands of years. They are mentioned in the Bible many times; the three Wise Men gave frankincense and myrrh to baby Jesus.

There are more than 200 references to aromatics, incense, and ointments throughout the Bible. Frankincense, myrrh, rosemary, cassia, and cinnamon essential oils were used for the anointing and healing of the sick.

Ancient Egyptians (4500 B.C.) used essential oils and aromatherapy for treating illness and performing rituals and religious ceremonies in temples and pyramids. Cedarwood, myrrh, and frankincense were and still are used in the embalming process.

Essential oils are created from the natural aromatic volatile liquids in plants (shrubs, flowers, trees, roots, bushes, and seeds). These liquids contain the life force of the plant. Pure, therapeutic-grade essential oils are best because they are distilled from plants. Anything less may not be effective and can, in some instances, be toxic. The purity of the oil and the therapeutic value will determine how they will work with your body.

According to Gary Young, "Thought equals frequency. Essential oils absorb our thoughts. They are registered in the oils as intent. Intent is directed energy. When you apply an intent-energized oil on your feet, they can saturate all of your cells within 60 seconds, stimulating creative thinking and pushing negative energy out of the cells, thus increasing the frequencies of the cells throughout the body. In that uplifted state, you can create a new desire to be better tomorrow. You have no limitations but those you choose to accept."[8]

Essential oils are used for aromatherapy, massage therapy, emotional health, personal care, nutritional supplements, household solutions, and much more. They have been used to kill harmful germs and to balance moods, lift spirits, and dispel negative emotions.

Young Living and doTerra are well-recognized therapeutic essential oils.

Exercise

According to the Centers for Disease Control and Prevention, regular exercise is important for maintaining a healthy weight and for reducing the risk of cardiovascular disease. One way to release weight is by reducing calories and increasing physical activity.[9] Another way is to release the emotions that caused the weight gain in the first place. Use the Trauma Release *(See Appendix, Tools for Health and Well-Being)* or the Emotion Code to help release stuck emotions.

Moderate exercise includes walking fast for 15 minutes, going for a bike ride, or cleaning the house two to three days a week. A more vigorous form of exercise would include jogging, running, swimming, and most types of competitive sports. Energize yourself!

Do it for your heart. Do it for you!

Grounding

To be grounded means to be rooted in the Earth. To maintain balance, we must be connected to Source/God and all of the Divine through the crown chakra at the top of the head and connected to Mother Earth through the feet.

Grounding helps to stay centered and focused. It helps to bring the body and mind back into the present moment. Here are a few ways to ground:

- Walk barefooted or lie on the ground
- Go for a walk or hug a tree
- Take a shower or bath
- Wear or carry a black tourmaline crystal

- Use an essential oil that helps with grounding
- Take a deep, cleansing breath in through the nose. Hold to a count of ten. Exhale through the mouth.
- Say out loud, "I Am grounded within the earth. I Am grounded within the earth. I Am grounded within the earth. And so it is uttered, and so it is done. Gratitude."
- Picture red roots coming from your feet, legs, and tail bone. Visualize them going deep down into the core of Mother Earth where there is golden white Light. The roots drink of this Light and bring this Light back up through the roots, into the body, and up to the heart where the Light runs through your circulatory system to every part of the body.

Herbal Remedies

Herbs have played an important role in man's history. They have been used for cooking and medicinal purposes. Herbs found their way into linen closets because of their pleasant fragrances, and they were used to dye homespun fabrics and leather. Herb gardens were an essential part of pioneer homes.

As more and more people become aware of the dangers of synthetic drugs and medications, herbal remedies are on the rise. Home remedies using herbs are considerably cheaper than prescription medicines and rarely have any side effects. Herbs can be easily grown outside in a garden or inside in a flower pot. Popular herbs to keep on hand are mint, chamomile, thyme, and lemon balm.

Mint, often used as a breath freshener, has been reported to help maintain a healthy digestive system and calm stomach aches. Ginger can help calm the stomach, ease the build-up of gases, and increase circulation.

Chamomile is perfect for relaxation and a good sleep; it can ease colic and anxiety issues. Thyme can help relieve stomach cramps due to gas build-up, and lemon balm has been used in the treatment of colds and the flu. Lemon balm can help to heal scrapes, minor cuts, and insect bites; it can also help with anxiety and insomnia.

Tiger balm, nutmeg oil, feverfew, passion flower, lemon balm, and peppermint oil work to help relieve headaches. Ginkgo biloba works to help improve circulation and reduce inflammation.

While most herbal remedies enhance the body's natural ability to heal through rebalancing and cleansing, there are some that can be dangerous when taken with synthetic medicine. Be sure to consult a knowledgeable practitioner before taking remedial herbs.

Herbal Teas

Herbal teas have been around for hundreds of years in Asia and are a natural healing drink that can be served hot or cold. There are sipping teas, and there are healing teas. Most teas have less caffeine than coffee. People are beginning to drink more teas like green tea, oolong tea, white tea, and black tea than coffee or soft drinks because of their medicinal purposes and pleasant flavor.

Traditional teas (such as green, black, white, and oolong teas) are made from the dried young leaves and leaf buds of the tea bush (Camelilia sinensis). Herbal teas are not made from the tea bush; they are made from an infusion of flowers, spices, herbs, leaves, seeds, bark, fruits, berries, spices, and plant roots.

Healing teas have medicinal properties that have been reported to cleanse and detoxify, alleviate pain, reduce fever, induce sweating, boost the immune system, fight infection, calm the stomach, fight cancer, ease spasms, support the heart and liver, cause vomiting, induce coughing to bring up phlegm, calm the nerves, help with insomnia, and much more. They work over a period of time.

Healing teas have been used in baths, as a poultice, and as a tincture. They can be a natural way to bring the body's internal systems back into balance.

"Live" Water vs. "Dead" Water

Mineral and spring water are considered "live" water because the life force of the water helps sustain our life force. Both contain electrolytes and other minerals that support all cellular functions.

Mineral water comes from a well or mineral spring and contains natural trace minerals important to maintaining well-being. The type of minerals in the water varies from region to region. Mineral water replaces minerals the body naturally loses through the day.

Spring water comes from underground aquifers. The water is clear and has been filtered by solid rock. It, too, contains natural minerals important to the body. Minerals improve the taste of the water.

Purified and distilled water are considered to be "dead" water because all contaminants have been removed, as well as electrolytes and minerals important to the body.

Purified water can come from any source of water, including spring, ground, or tap water. The EPA requires that it meet significantly higher filtration and purification standards than those for regular drinking water (such as tap water).

Distilled water is water that has been through a distillation process. It is ideal for applications where minerals can be counterproductive (for example, machinery and cleaning products). While distilled water is the cleanest bottled water readily available, it is not good for drinking because it pulls minerals out of the bloodstream and other parts of the body.

Muscle Testing

Muscle testing is used by chiropractors, acupuncturists, and energy practitioners to test the body. Anyone can use it. The body will never lie to you. Use it to learn what is good for your body and to get answers about your body. Use it to find out if a product is for your very best and highest good.

When you ask your body a yes-or-no question, it will respond one way for a "yes," and another way for a "no." The body will remain strong when the answer is "yes" and weaken when the answer is "no." Negative words or thoughts weaken our energy field.

The best way to muscle test is to close the eyes, the entrance to the soul and your inner guidance, to keep the mind from overriding and manipulating the answer.

Test to determine if a supplement is for your very best and highest good and what dosage you should take. For example, you may need vitamin C while treating the common cold, but you may not need it when you are well again. Muscle test to be sure the brand will be beneficial for you.

Muscle test to better understand what is causing pain

or dis-ease in the body. Muscle test to see if you are ready to release it and what you should do to release it. People begin to get better when they get sick and tired of being sick and tired. As long as we are getting something out of our dis-ease, we still need it; such as attention, identity (we do not know who we are without it), karma, etc.

You can test for anything; just be ready for the answer. It may not always be what you wanted it would be.

There are many different ways to muscle test. Two of the most common are:

Sway Test: Your body is a crystal that can be used as a pendulum. Stand straight with your eyes closed. The eyes are the entranceway to the soul. Your mind can manipulate the answer if your eyes are open. Ask your body to show you a "yes." Your body will most likely sway forward or backward. Ask your body to show you a "no." Your body will most likely sway the opposite direction. Now ask your question to find your answer. If you would like to know if a particular product is for your very best and highest good, hold it to your waist, then ask the question.

"O" Ring: Make a circle by putting your thumb and index finger together. Do the same with the other thumb and index finger, interlocking the two circles together. Ask your body to show you a "yes," then try to pull the circles apart. Ask your body to show you a "no," then try to pull the circles apart. The circles should break apart with one of the answers. You will know the difference between a "yes" and "no" answer.

Always ask your body to show you a "yes" and a "no" before starting. If you don't test the body first, the answer received most likely be reversed and you will not know this. The body typically pulls forward for a "yes" and backward for a "no." If your body pulls in the opposite directions, your polarity may be off because you are dehydrated. Drink a full glass of water, and then try again in five minutes.

Now ask your question to find your answer. Ask "would it be for my very best and highest good to..." Phrasing your question this way will not take away free will; you decide whether or not you should do something. Your body may not answer you if you ask, "should I..." because it takes away free will.

Make sure you are grounded (eat nuts or dark chocolate). If you still cannot get a good answer, check your belief system (you may not believe muscle testing is possible) or rephrase the question. For example, begin your question with "Would it be for my very best and highest good to..." You may have a belief out of alignment or you may be asking a question that takes away free will.

Processed Foods vs. Whole Foods

Processed foods are put through a "process," produced in a manufacturing plant, packaged, and then put on a shelf to be stored until ready to be eaten. They contain artificial ingredients (preservatives, oils, sweeteners, and flavors) to enhance taste and to prolong shelf life. Cooking time is minimal or none. Ingredients include chemicals and other unrecognizable names. If you can't pronounce an ingredient or you don't know what it is, you probably shouldn't be eating it.

Natural or whole foods are grown in orchards, gardens, or greenhouses. They are unprocessed, unrefined, and have a shorter shelf life because they have no artificial ingredients. They are full of vitamins, minerals, antioxidants, phytochemicals, and fiber your body needs to be healthy. The life force in plants helps sustain our life force. Cooking them takes more time, but they are good for the body and soul.

The main difference between the two is Love. Love cannot be found in processed foods (machine-made). The more one loves to cook, the greater the love put into the food (home-made). Love makes food taste better. Homemade food fuels the physical body, and the love put into making the food fuels the soul.

Raise Self-Esteem

A Gift to Help: Low-Esteem Blocker Kit
The following is an excerpt from *The Sapiential Discourses – Universal Wisdom, by All There Is, Was, and Ever Shall Be* through Elliott Eli Jackson, Chapter 1 – "The Self Revealed"):

"Put together a low self-esteem blocker kit. If you are prone to bouts of low self-esteem, do the following:

- Have a list of close friends, those people you can call or email quickly.
- Call or email the individuals on your list and ask them to give you at least seven good qualities about yourself. Explain to them what you are doing. And remember, true friends will not hesitate to assist you.
- Ask them also to email or mail the list to you so you can view it when you are feeling down.
- When you receive them, put them in your kit.
- Each time you receive or hear something positive directed to you, from any source, write it down and place it in your kit also.
- Make some notes of the positive statements you received about yourself with the names of the people who said them on the notes. Hang them around your house—for example, in the bathroom, kitchen, or office.

- Make a list of ten positive personal affirmations and repeat them to yourself twice a day.

"We tell you, if you do these things, along with meditation, prayer, and faith, whenever and wherever lower-vibrational influences make attempts to interject negativity into the mental portion of your being, you will be able to counteract the attempts. This may seem simple, but everything involving the spirit/soul is. Everything involving the spirit/soul is connected to the spirits/souls of others and the spirit of the universe, which is us, the we!

"It is imperative to note that the concept of negativity is not natural. Remember, you are love! Unhappiness is not in your makeup. It has been created by the human mental and reinforced by the emotional." [10]

Release Stress

A few ways to release stress, especially in the workplace, are to:
- Play harp, flute, or classical music in the background—allow yourself to connect with the music to keep the flow of energy moving through you and to prevent energy from getting stuck
- Breathe—allow your soul to reconnect with the breath of God
- Meditate—take 5-10 minutes to clear your mind

- Take a break and stretch—take time to disconnect and re-center yourself
- Yoga

Self-Healing Techniques

There are times when we need help with healing and for this we should always seek help, but there are also techniques we can use to heal ourselves.

Creative Visualization

Close your eyes and visualize emerald green healing light coming in through your crown chakra, down into your head, and watch it go through every part of your body, down to your feet. The green light moves through each one of your chakras and out into your energy field. Hold that vision, watching the green healing light move through you to heal and re-energize every part of your being.

Close your eyes and visualize emerald green healing light coming into the afflicted body part. See the body part healed. Know it to be true. Do this as often as necessary.

Request Help from Angels and Guides

Before going to bed at night, ask your angels and spirit guides to take you to the Jade Temple for healing while you sleep.

Talk to Your Body

Everything in life has a consciousness, including your body. Talk to it. Tell it how grateful you are for all that it has done for you. Apologize for any trauma you have stored in that body part. Tell the body part it is time to heal, and you wish to help with its healing. Allow yourself to release the stored trauma. See the body part fully healed. Believe the body part is healing so the healing can take place. Anything is possible. The sky's the limit!

Thump the Thymus

Thump your thymus to center yourself and bring you back into balance. The thymus is a spiritual organ. Many women, especially the elderly, instinctively know to do this when something in life takes their breath away. They do this involuntarily.

Trauma Release

Decide what you would like to release. Set your intention to release "everything from past lives, present life, and future lives, going back to the root wherever it started." Then place one hand across the forehead and the other hand across the back of the skull at the nape of the neck (base of the occipital bone). Hold your hands in place and bring up (remember) the trauma. Allow your body to release in whatever way it desires.

Your head may go in circles or rock back and forth (nurturing the inner child); lean to the left or lean to the right. The left side of the body represents the past; the right side, the current time. You may cry, or your body may twitch or tremble. Your head may go backwards (exasperation), or it may go down. The farther down the head goes, the more deeply rooted the trauma.

No matter what happens, keep your hands in place and allow the body to release. You will know you are done when you experience a deep, involuntary breath. If the breath is not deep, repeat again at a later time. You are not yet ready to release it all. Peel back the many layers so you can get to the core of the trauma.

You can also place two drops each of Young Living's Release essential oil into the palm of your hands, and then rub your hands together. Inhale deeply three times; release through the mouth. Now use the trauma release. Using Release essential oil will help to release whatever it is you no longer need.

You can perform this procedure on other people, including children.

Other Techniques
Other self-healing techniques include: the Emotional Freedom Technique (EFT), the Tapas Acupressure Technique (TAT), and the Emotion Code.

White Dove Circle of Light and Love in Springboro, Ohio, teaches these techniques. You can also search the internet for more information.

Setting Personal Boundaries

> *"The relationships you have with others are a reflection of the vibration you offer. There aren't actually any 'others;' it's actually all about the relationship you have with yourself. They are projections of that. You can change the people, and new ones will appear with the same dynamics. But it's changing your emotions (vibration) that changes the dynamics—whether with the same people, or new people."* ~ Abraham-Hicks

Personal boundaries in relationships are very important. We teach people how we want to be treated by what we allow, what we stop, and what we reinforce. Boundaries are a sign of respect. They say you respect yourself, and others respect you, too.

Boundaries are for your protection. They should have consequences (cause and effect). Consequences should be fair and enforced. There is no reason to set a boundary if it will not be enforced. The situation will only worsen because your words become meaningless.

Without healthy boundaries, we allow people to take advantage of us. Co-dependent relationships have no boundaries because both partners believe they cannot live without the other.

A co-dependent relationship is a pattern of behavior wherein one partner makes sacrifices, real or imagined, for the other partner's happiness, looking for approval. They give endless support to their partner, even at the cost of their own mental, emotional, and physical health.

The receiving (weaker) partner depends on the giving (stronger) partner for just about everything from caregiving to bill paying to making meals and running errands. Physical, mental, and emotional control are exerted over the receiving partner because the receiving partner is afraid the giving partner will leave them. The giving partner is often criticizing, overbearing, and demanding one minute and loving the next.

At the time the receiving partner feels a sense of purpose and may appear to be self-sacrificing when in reality they may be avoiding their own unhappiness and personal issues. Eventually they lose their self-worth, thereby lowering their self-esteem. The receiving partner believes they are not getting much in return, but they really are getting something (e.g., financial security, shared religious or political beliefs, etc.) out of the situation or they wouldn't stay in the relationship.

In a co-dependent relationship, both parties are getting something from the other for fulfillment, even if it doesn't appear that way on the surface. Look deeper. As long as both parties are getting something out of the relationship, they will be together. If the relationship is karmic, both parties must stay together until the karmic debt is balanced. If the relationship is healthy and loving when the debt is balanced, stay in it. If no love exists when the debt is over, leave. More karma is created by staying in the relationship than by leaving. This newly-created karma must then have to be balanced.

People who lack boundaries have low self-esteem. They cannot communicate directly and honestly. They become dependent on others, being controlled and manipulated by how others think, feel, and act toward them. They are fearful of rejection and conflict. They often have an inner child that needs healing. A person without boundaries cannot love him or herself.

Healthy relationships are not possible without proper communication. Tell people how you feel, and listen to them when they talk about their feelings. Compromise can bring an out-of-balance relationship back into balance.

How you handle the relationship is important. Empower yourself; stop saying "yes" when you mean "no." Express what you feel. It's not what you say but how you say it that counts. Timing is important. When one person is on the defense, no one wins. Diffuse the situation, and then speak your truth so compromise and change can take place.

Take Time for You

As the saying goes, if you do not take time for you, no one else will.

Take time to pray and meditate. Take time to eat healthy and take any appropriate supplements (always muscle test to see what your body needs). Take time to exercise.

Take time for a stroll in the park, to smell the flowers, and to soak in the bathtub (using therapeutic essential oils). Take time for a manicure or a pedicure; better yet, let someone else do it for you. Take time for a game of golf or a day at the beach.

Take time to laugh; laughter is the best medicine. Laughter helps to release stress; it will prolong your life.

The Attitude of Gratitude

Gratitude is the highest form of prayer there is. Give gratitude in advance for what you would like to receive; it shows you have faith that your request will be granted.

To create more of what you want in life, give gratitude for what you have. Give gratitude for having the money to pay bills, to put food on the table and clothes on your back. Give gratitude for good health, good friends, and for those who love and accept you as you are. Give gratitude in advance for what you want to happen, such as healing.

Three to five minutes of gratitude can help shift a negative way of thinking into a positive one. It can turn a bad day into a good one.

Give gratitude for the many blessings received in life, especially those not recognized. And remember to give gratitude for the many lessons in life for they helped to create the beautiful person you are today.

We always have what we need. We get into trouble when we want for more than we need!

The Importance of a Good Cleanse

The human body should be purged periodically of the many chemicals and minerals for which it should have only trace, if any, amounts. An excess of toxins can slow down the mind, body, and spirit; it can inhibit well-being.

Fasting to cleanse the body should only be done on a limited basis (once or twice a year) for no more than three days. Anything more can be detrimental to your health. During this time, drink only water and eat only small portions of raw vegetables to cleanse the blood and to aid your digestive system by removing unnecessary particles that need to be removed.

The Importance of a Well-Balanced Diet

A well-balanced diet provides the energy needed to make it through the day. It consists of all the vitamins, minerals, and nutrients essential to maintain a healthy body. A well-balanced diet supports the cardiovascular and immune systems and assists in weight control. The overall benefit is the feeling of well-being.

Foods should be organic and fresh, free of chemicals and preservatives. Whole grains (not processed grains), beans, and nuts should be eaten. More fish, fowl, and lamb should be eaten than red meats. Leafy, green vegetables (raw or steamed) and fruits should be eaten daily.

Milk should be included for calcium and protein. Foods should be rich in Vitamins A, C, and E; selenium; potassium; and fiber. Fried foods and an overabundance of sugars and alcohol should be avoided.

A well-balanced diet provides all the vitamins and minerals, calcium and protein necessary to support healthy cells, organs, and muscle tissue. A strong, healthy body makes it difficult for dis-ease to settle in.

The Importance of Nutrition

The human body is comprised of ten complex systems, each performing a different function to regulate the body: skeletal, muscular, nervous, endocrine, cardiovascular, lymphatic, respiratory, digestive, urinary, and reproductive.

There are six basic elements that make up the physical body: carbon, nitrogen, hydrogen, calcium, oxygen, and phosphorus. Other elements (in miniscule amounts) include: sodium, magnesium, sulfur, zinc, copper, molybdenum, selenium, chlorine, iodine, fluorine, cobalt, iron, manganese, lead, lithium, aluminum, strontium, silicon, arsenic, bromine, and vanadium.

Nutrition means eating a healthy diet, full of the nutrients found in fruits and vegetables grown in fertile soil. Four essential nutrients that make up the cornerstones of a healthy diet that keep the physical body in balance and functioning well: water, carbohydrates, fat, and protein.

- Carbohydrates found in plant foods get converted into glucose, providing energy for the physical body.
- Excessive fats cause problems in the body, but a reasonable amount of fat is required to support growth and to provide energy.
- Proteins can be found in meat, fish, eggs, nuts, seeds, and dairy products. They support the muscles, tissues, skin, and major organs.

When we feel positive and loving, we eat healthily (fresh fruits and vegetables, beans, and whole grains). When we feel lousy and think negatively, we tend to eat poorly (fried foods, unnatural foods, and sweets).

The foods we choose to eat and how we prepare our

food will determine how well they will be assimilated in the body. Natural foods contribute to optimum health and longevity of the body.

The Proper Amount of Hydration

The most common substance found on earth is water. Every living thing requires water to survive. The human body is made up of mostly water.

Water is important for the body for hydration and digestion, for our teeth and bones. Water is important to flush the body of chemicals, toxins, and other waste products it contains. It regulates body temperature and maintains cleanliness by excreting urine and other poisonous substances from the body. It serves as a lubricant for the body, aiding in chewing, swallowing, and moving solids through the body. Water is the best cure for most illnesses.

Because the human body is approximately 70 to 90 percent water, most people (unless dehydrated) only need to drink four to six cups a day or the body will become oversaturated. Floppy fat is a sign of too much water in the body. The body can only process so much at a time, fluid or solid.

Just as too little water can lead to dehydration, too much water can cause mineral depletion and other imbalances within the body. Too much water can dilute stomach acids, causing acid reflux, and agitate a hiatal hernia. Too much water combined with a high-fiber diet can lead to bloating, gas, and other digestive disorders.

Tools for Clearing and Protection

Cutting Cords of Attachment

While in the womb, the umbilical cord connects the developing fetus to its mother. Its function is to supply oxygen, deliver nutrients, and withdraw blood rich in carbon dioxide and depleted in nutrients to the fetus.[11]

An ethereal or etheric cord is an energetic cord in the spirit realm that connects one person to another. It is a way to tap into another's energy. Have you ever thought of a friend and then that person called you? A cord went out and your friend received your thought through the cord.

Etheric cords can be anywhere on your spirit body or energy field, although they are usually found in the solar plexus (stomach) area of the body. Cords between romantic partners are usually found in the sacral (between the hips) area of the body. Cords can strengthen over time. The more you connect with someone, the stronger the cord becomes. Energy flows in both directions. An ache or pain in the mid-section of the body (a back ache, for example) can be the result of a cord. Cut the cord!

Cords can suck your energy. We all have that friend

who does all the talking while you do all the listening. Your energy becomes drained just listening to them! Energy is only flowing in one direction. Remove the cord so this person will stop draining your energy.

Cords can also be created to psychically attack someone. Someone intentionally tries to steal another's power, leaving them to feel physically, mentally, and emotionally drained. Cords must be removed to maintain health and well-being and clarity of mind.

To protect yourself from being corded into while talking with someone, try the following:

- When you notice your shoulders begin to slump and your mind begins to wander, end the conversation. Tell the person you are talking to you have to go to the bathroom. Wait 10 minutes to call them back. Usually what this person was talking about is no longer important. Unconsciously, this person's main reason for calling was to suck your energy because their energy level needed refueling. When you end the conversation, cut the cord.
- Bring your feet together, interlace your fingers and place them across your stomach, bring your elbows in. Hold this pose as long as necessary. By doing this, a protective shield is created so this person cannot tap into your energy.

To remove cords:
- Visualize a Platinum Flame. Pull the cord from you and place the end in the Platinum Flame to be transmuted. Then pull the cord from the person who corded into you and place it in the Platinum Flame. Put the entire cord into the Platinum Flame.

To release a loved one that has crossed over, an ex-lover or friend, write a Release Letter and burn it (purification) so both parties can move forward to the next stage of their evolutionary journey. Release any cords.

Release letters are important. They remove "the tie that binds" so you can both move forward on your evolutionary journey. *(See Tools for Spiritual Growth: Release Letters)*

Help with Challenging People and Situations

Life can be challenging from time to time, dealing with difficult people and situations. What the world needs more of is love. So why not send love to help ease a situation?!

Namaste!

The Sanskrit word "Namaste" means "May the Christ in me meet the Christ in you." It means "My soul honors your soul."

Close your eyes and picture the person involved in your mind's eye and say out loud or through thought,

"Namaste!" You are asking this person to meet you on a higher level of love. They can't be mean to you. If they can't be nice, they'll stay away...and that's okay.

The Christ or Higher Self is pure unconditional love. It knows no fear or negativity. Use "Namaste" when you travel, shop, or go out to eat to attract helpful, pleasant people. Write the word on a piece of paper and place it in your suitcase. Set the intention for your luggage to arrive with you and without damage.

Wearing "Namaste" jewelry carries the energy of the word with you wherever you go.

Use the "Namaste" daily so life will flow with ease and grace.

Talk to Their Higher Self

If you would like to get your point across to someone who is closed-minded, picture the person in your mind's eye and state your case. Then ask—never demand—what you would like to achieve. To demand something of someone's higher self is to take away their free will. Never take away someone's free will! It is a misuse of energy and will create karma.

Always ask for the very best and highest good for all concerned. Then allow life to take place. Keep in mind, sometimes what you asked for was for your very best and highest good, even though it wasn't what you wanted. Trust that as times goes on, you will understand why.

Send Unconditional Love

The only thing that heals is love. Magenta is the color of pure unconditional love. It is nurturing and compassionate. Surrounding someone in Magenta Light helps to soften them so they will be more receptive to your request.

Surround yourself and your loved ones in Magenta Light daily to help keep low-vibration entities away. These fallen angels are taught by their leaders that nurturing and compassion are not good. They want only the wisdom and energy with White Light. They do not want that "touchy, feely stuff." It repels them.

Use it daily to clear spaces where low-vibration people live; for example, a crack house or a residence with someone that makes you feel uncomfortable. Over time, these low-vibration people will move out and loving tenants will move in. This is something I personally witnessed. After one month of visualizing the Magenta Light through a shady man living in a nearby house, he was gone. The new tenants moving in were a loving couple engaged to be married. It really does work!

Releasing Low Vibration Entities

Signs that you have an entity on you, draining your energy: exhaustion for no reason, depression, yawning all the time even though you slept well the night before, grumpy attitude, thinking/acting negatively (out of character), a stiff neck, an ache or pain that moves around body.

These low-vibration entities attach themselves to your weakest areas and along the "T" line of the back (neck, shoulders, and spine). Anxiety and depression, bipolar and schizophrenia are all signs of low-vibration entities. Be aware of your energy at all times!

A mantra using Young Living's Release essential oil to remove low-vibration entities:

Place two drops each of Release into the palm of your hands, and then rub your hands together. Take three deep breaths, breathing in through the nose and out through the mouth. Say out loud:

"In the Name of All There Is, Was, and Ever Shall Be, I command all lower vibrational portions of the universe that are within, on, and around me in any other measure than as assigned by the universe, even in trace amounts, to leave me now, to leave my aura, my energy field, my mental, and my emotional. I further command you to leave the land that this building is on and every crack and crevice of my abode, away from my finances, my ability to intake money and pay my bills, and away from my other, my parents, my children and grandchildren, their auras and energy field. And so it is uttered, and so it is done."

Know it is done. BELIEVE it is done!

If you feel you have one or more spirits (yes, you can have more than one!) on you or in your energy field, say out loud, as necessary:

"In the name of All There Is, Was, and Ever Shall Be, I command lower vibrational portions of the All that are within, on, and around me in any other measure other than that as naturally assigned by the universe to leave. I send you away to your proper place of existence, which is not on this person, in this home, or on this land. And so it is uttered, so it is done!"

BELIEVE it is done, and it shall be.

When finished, you may notice yourself taking a deep breath—a sign you have released them. You may feel "lighter." Recite either mantra daily to keep lower-vibrational spirits away. If your words get twisted or omitted while saying the mantra, this is the lower-vibrations affecting you. Repeat the mantra meaningfully until you can say it clearly.

Use the following method if you want to feel and release a low-vibration entity:

Visualize God's Divine Light and Love as a pool of White Light. Ask the low-vibrations to go to the Light.

If they do not go, command them to go by saying, "If there are any entities within, on, or around me that are not of the highest Light and Love, I COMMAND YOU in the Name of All that is Holy and Pure to present yourself to me now. You are not welcome here." If you cannot say "in the Name of All that is Holy and Pure" clearly, you have a low-vibration entity on you.

Wait a few seconds to get their attention, and then say, "If there are any entities within, on, or around me that are not of the highest Light and Love, I COMMAND YOU in the Name of All that is Holy and Pure to move to my left arm now. You are not welcome here."

Wait a few seconds to give them time to move to your left arm, and then say, "If there are any entities within, on, or around me that are not of the highest Light and Love, I COMMAND YOU in the Name of All that is Holy and Pure to move to my left hand now. You are not welcome here."

If there is an entity, you will feel its energy in your hand. It may feel heavy, moist, tingly, whatever. You will feel it.

Once you feel them in your hand, say again, "If there are any entities within, on, or around me that are not of the highest Light and Love, I COMMAND YOU in the Name of All that is Holy and Pure to move into this pool of God's White Light and Divine Love."

Shake them off into the pool of God's Divine Love and Light you created, putting your hand into the Light to shake them off.

If they do not go, peel them off and put them into the Light. Flood your body with Magenta Light from your head to your feet.

You may have to repeat this procedure several times if you feel you have more entities on you. It is not unusual to have many.

Other Methods

Smudge yourself or someone else from head to toe, front and back, with cedar to clear, followed by sage to seal and protect.

Put a drop of eucalyptus oil on the top of your head, third eye, throat, each wrist, and the tops of your feet to keep low vibration entities away. They really don't like this essential oil!

Space Clearing

Space clearing is an art practiced in many ancient cultures. Just as dust and dirt accumulates in your home physically, the same happens with someone else's energy on an energetic level. You may not see the "dust and dirt" of human emotions, but they do accumulate in the spirit realm. Clear them out periodically.

When you get up out of a chair, some of your energy is left behind. The more you sit in the chair, the more your energy collects in that chair. It becomes comfortable because it has your energy in it. The same goes for a favorite blanket, article of clothing, or side of bed. Bring a favorite blanket of yours with you when you travel. Sleep with it for a better night's rest. Hotel beds have many other people's energy in them. That why we don't always sleep well in them.

Clear your home at least once or twice a year, especially

after a major trauma has taken place, such as death or divorce. It is also important to clear a house you have just moved into, especially if the house was in foreclosure. Estate jewelry or inherited items should always be cleared before using to release any unwanted energy.

Experiment with different ways to find what works best for you. Here are a few methods to space clear:

Candles: Candles invoke the energy of purification and inspiration. They help to release stress. Their aroma is uplifting.

Herbs: Fresh herbs such as sage, cedar, fir, eucalyptus, and lavender can be used to purify energy. To keep low-vibration entities away, decorate a room or house with fresh eucalyptus in every room.

Incense: Use a natural, high-quality incense to freshen the air and calm the energy of your space. Cedar incense helps to clear negative or stale energy.

Essential Oils: Diffuse lavender, eucalyptus, lemon, mint, lemongrass, or wild orange to clear a space while, at the same time, providing beautiful aromatherapy.

Music and Nature Sounds: Sounds can also clear the energy of a space, our mood, and our well-being. Playing high-vibrational, classic, or Native American flute music can shift your energy to find peace within. Place a bird feeder outside of your home. The sound of birds chirping helps to clear negative energy. That's why there are so many birds around hospitals and care centers.

Tibetan Bells or Crystal Singing Bowls: These bowls not only clear energy, they bring a powerful healing quality for those in the room. Take a bell over your head to clear you.

Crystals: Crystals can raise the vibration of a room while strengthening your own energy.

Fresh Flowers: Flowers are of a high vibration and can bring the energy of beauty, harmony, and joyfulness to any space.

Smudging

Smudging a home is always a good idea to clear stale or negative energy and low-vibration entities. You can also smudge a person or an item. The term "smudging" comes from the Native American shamanic traditions of clearing energy, although every culture has its own way of smudging. Smudging helps strengthen well-being. The smoke from the herbs unleashes the healing energy of the plant to neutralize and purify any negative presence.

When smudging, it is best to use cedar for clearing and

sage to seal and protect. In olden days, a handful of cedar was thrown into the fire or onto a wood stove to clear the energy and musty smells in the room.

Place the dried cedar in an abalone shell or fireproof pan. Light the cedar so it begins to burn. Once the fire gets going, blow it out. It is the smoke you want because smoke goes everywhere. Using a feather or your hand, take the smoke around the outside of the house first, then the inside.

Inside the house, smudge each room, including closets, bathrooms, and basements. Open drawers, cabinets, appliances, etc. Send around doors, windows, mirrors, computer monitors and television screens.

Test to see if the room is clear by using a bell. If it is clear, the sound will bounce around the room and the tone will vibrate longer with each ring. Ring the bell over your head to bring you back into balance.

Once the rooms are clear, use sage in the same way to seal and protect the space.

The Platinum Shield

The Platinum Shield is a seal, a cover, a protection. In order to call this universal shield upon oneself, do the following:
- Center yourself
- Take a deep breath
- Exclaim the following from your being – Out Loud!

In the name of All There Is, Was and Ever Shall Be,
I call upon the universal Platinum Shield of Light.
I call upon the Platinum Shield to come upon my very being.
I call upon the Platinum Shield to cover me.
I call upon the Platinum Shield to protect me.
I call upon the Platinum Shield to hover over and around me.
I call upon the Platinum Shield to stand beside me.
I call upon the Platinum Shield to hold me up from my base.

I fully acknowledge the need for my shield's presence in my life now.
I fully recognize my shield's power as given to it from the Source of all things.
Mighty Platinum Shield, cover me from head to toe.
Shield me from all that is not in my highest good.
Protect me from disease, stress, worry and pain.
Shield me from all my personal addictions, for I do have some.
Shield me from those things that I need not be exposed to.
Come upon me in a mighty way,
Charge through my being,

Push away from me all that should not be in or around my being,
Let your power enfold me.
Send away from me all negative aspects of our great universes,
Intensely protect me.

From the power within me that comes from Source/God, I call thee.
I need thee, my shield,
Source/God has given you unto me – Come!

Protect me from all darkness,
Keep me in light and love.
Keep the darkness of my species away from me and mine.
Shoot in all directions from my being,
Protect those in my bloodline,
Protect those that are of a high vibration like me, seeking peace on Earth.
Platinum Shield be placed upon my chest,
Protect my heart of hearts,
Protect my soul.
Shield my mental from low thoughts and my being from low actions.
Cover me.

*So it is uttered – So it is done!
Perfection I AM. Perfection I will be!
Now my Shield protects me.*

This tool WE give unto thee. It is for the use of woman and mankind. Remember WE love you! ~ Source/God through Elliott Eli Jackson

Tools for Spiritual Growth

Beauty Raises Energy

Just in case no one told you today, you are good enough. ~ Anonymous

Surround yourself with Beauty! It will uplift your spirit and raise your vibration.

Everyone loves to be surrounded by beauty, e.g., beautiful clothes, jewelry, artwork, flowers, music. Surround yourself with nature. Treat yourself to expensive candles, or play beautiful, soothing music. Place crystals in different rooms of your house. Diffuse essential oils. Make your surroundings at home and work more beautiful and radiant. A few small, inexpensive things can make a big difference in the way you feel.

Do something for yourself that inspires beauty. Drink tea out of a beautiful china cup with a silver spoon. Eat dinner by candlelight to create mystery and ambiance. A simple vase of flowers can be uplifting; the aromatherapy alone is soothing and healing. Put sachets in your closets and drawers so your clothes always smell good. Use incense or diffuse essential oils. Dance!

Everyone loves to feel beautiful. Buy a new outfit that makes you feel good or get a makeover. Wear a perfume that smells beautiful. Get your hair done, a massage or a Reiki session, a manicure, or a pedicure. Take a bath with essential oils and sea salts for a relaxing end of the day.

True beauty comes from within. When you feel beautiful inside, everyone else will see the beauty in you on the outside as well!

Codes of Conduct for a Disciple of the Holy Spirit

The following discourse is from the Maha Chohan (Great Divine Director) as written in *The Ascension Flame of Purification and Immortality* by Aurelia Louise Jones:[12]

- Become conscious always of your aspiration to embody the full expression of Godhood, and devote all of thy being and thy service to that end.
- Learn the lessons of harmlessness; neither by word nor thought, nor feeling will you ever inflict evil upon any part of Life. Know that action and physical violence will keep you in the realm of pain, suffering, and mortality.
- Stir not a brother's sea of emotion thoughtlessly or deliberately. Know the storm in which you would place his spirit will sooner or later flow upon the banks of your own life stream. Rather

bring always tranquility, love, harmony, and peace to all life.
- Disassociate yourself from the personal and planetary delusion. Never allow yourself to love your little self more than the harmony of the universe. If you are right, there is no need to acclaim it. If you are wrong, apologize.
- Walk gently upon the Earth and through the universe, knowing that the body is a sacred temple, in which dwells the Holy Spirit, bringing peace and illumination to life everywhere. Keep your temple always in a respectful and purified manner, as befitting the habitation of the Spirit of Love and Truth. Respect and honor with gentle dignity all other temples, knowing that often within a crude exterior burns a great light.
- In the presence of Nature, absorb the beauties and gifts of Her kingdoms in gentle gratitude. Do not desecrate Her by vile thoughts, sounds, or emotions, or by physical acts that despoil Her virgin beauty. Honor the Earth, "the Mother" that is hosting your evolutionary pathway.
- Do not form nor offer opinions unless invited to do so, and then, only after prayer and silent invocation for guidance. Speak when God chooses to

- say something through you. At other times it is best to speak little, or to remain peacefully silent.
- Let your heart sing a song of gratitude and joy unto God. Be grateful always for all that you have received and that you have in the now moment. Tap in to the River of Life, River of Love and Abundance that lies within the Sacred Heart.
- In speech and action be gentle, but with the dignity that always accompanies the Presence of the living God that lives within the temple of your being. Constantly place all the faculties of your being and all the inner unfoldment of your nature at the feet of the God-power, endeavoring to manifest the perfection of compassion when meeting those in distress.
- Let your word be spoken in gentleness, humility, and loving service. Do not allow the impression of humility to be mistaken for lethargy, for the servant of the Lord, like the sun in the heavens, is eternally vigilant and constantly outpouring the gifts of Love to those who open their hearts to receive them.

Decrees

Affirmations work to create a condition or modify a behavior as long as the belief is in agreement with the affirmation.

When the two are not in agreement, we stop saying the affirmation, thus stopping the process.

Decrees are more powerful because we call on God, the Great I AM, to help create a condition or modify our behavior. A decree always begins with the words "I Am."

Source/God has given mankind a discourse of Great I Am decrees that, "if stated and followed without prejudices, along with an open-mind, will change the claimer's life and the direction of your world."[13]

Following is an excerpt from *The Sapiential Discourses – Universal Wisdom Book III, by All There Is, Was, and Ever Shall Be* through Elliott Eli Jackson, Chapter 1 – The Great I AM, "Mankind's I Am Decrees" section:

1. *I Am, You Are, WE are One*
I AM one with all things. I AM one with God. I AM God in human form. I AM one with all humans and all humans are one with God. I AM one with the Earth on which I dwell. I AM one with all portions of Earth—the air, the water, the fire, and the wind. I AM the air, the water, the fire, and the wind. I AM one with all animals and sea dwellers. I AM one with all portions of Earth. I AM one with the oceans; I AM the oceans. I AM one with the rivers; I AM the rivers. I AM one with the mountains and the hills; I AM the mountains and the hills. I AM one with the grass and the dew; I AM the grass and the dew. I AM one with the rain and

the snow; I AM the rain and the snow. I AM one with everything and everyone. I AM everything and everyone. I AM and can never be separate from self, from God. I AM divine. I AM eternal. I AM everlasting spirit, everlasting soul. I AM from the beginning to the end. I AM that which I AM and can be nothing else. So it is uttered, so it is.

2. *I AM Perfect*
I AM amongst the perfect ones. I AM perfect just as I AM. At each stage of my life I was perfect—seven perfect systems in synchronization with everything everywhere. I AM majestic. I AM regal. I AM powerful. I AM able to achieve that which I desire. I AM beautiful. I AM wonderful. I AM true. I AM honest. I AM magnificent. I AM glorious. I AM confident. I AM able to move all obstructions from my path. I AM capable and able. I AM civic. I AM intellect. I AM binary. I AM operational. I AM inspirational. I AM tough. I AM model of the universes. I AM quantum. I AM troubadour. I AM humble of the Earth. I AM philosopher. I AM scholar. I AM torch and bearer of Light and Love. I AM Light and Love in perfect human form. So it is uttered, so it is.

3. *I AM Creator*
There is nothing I cannot do. I AM provider. I can provide for self and any others that I wish or desire to. I AM

obtainer. There is nothing I cannot obtain if I but wish or desire to. I AM shaper of myself. I AM able to cause myself to be that which I desire to be. I AM former of self. No one causes me to be save self. I AM captain of my own ship, which includes relationships. I AM captain of self. I AM dream maker. I AM able to take my dreams and desires and bring them into reality. I AM Creator. I Create. So it is uttered, so it is.

4. I AM Master

I AM image of God on Earth. I can master all that I desire. I AM able to acquire all information necessary for me to achieve anything. I AM a seeker. I AM a teacher. I AM great in and of myself. I AM not an island. I AM communal. I AM able to isolate from others when the need arises to collect myself, reflect upon my previous actions, behaviors, and decisions, and then reintroduce or reintegrate myself back into society at a higher vibration than I was previous to the self-imposed isolation. I AM fluent in speech and projection. I AM orator and professor to self and others. I AM Master and Master I shall be. So it is uttered, so it is.

5. I Am Disciple

I AM a disciple of life. I AM able to learn or remember from my mis-takes. I AM listener to all without judgment. I AM not prone to contempt prior to investigation as I was before. I AM a discerner of truth. I AM watcher. I AM able to observe and take in that which I need to improve myself. I AM open-minded. I AM capable of reading and writing. I AM able to voice my opinion without anger. I AM able to control my temper always. I AM capable of being passionate without being aggressive or submissive. I AM well-rounded and centered. I AM non-judgmental yet observational. I AM studious, able to pass all scholastic, professional or any other test placed before me by man to show my level of competency. I AM attentive to all. I AM remembering and growing in each given moment. So it is uttered, so it is.

6. *I AM Energy*
I AM body in motion. I AM able to do all the physical tasks necessary for self. I AM able to push away and out any restriction that may come upon or within my physical being, often with the assistance of my others. I AM able to send Light and Love outside of my being to my others, to places and spaces on Earth and beyond. I AM a most positive effect on the human stream of consciousness. I AM as healthy as I cause myself to be. I AM able to understand that I can heal myself. I AM atomic energy. I AM rejuvenating right now. I AM of healthy cells. I AM whole. I AM abundantly filled with power. I AM the energy of the universes. So it is uttered, so it is.

7. I AM Action

I AM able to get things done. I AM unstoppable. I AM unmovable when I must be yet movable when I need to be. I AM walking 10,000 steps each day on Earth. I AM sitting only when I need to rest, otherwise I AM moving. I AM a go-getter. I AM not to wait for opportunities to come to me; I AM going to them. I AM seeking truth at all times. I AM seeking the information that I need to improve self and assist others. I AM action propelled by self. So it is uttered, so it is.

8. I AM Self-sustaining

I AM able to take care of self. This includes my body, mind and spirit. I AM taking all of the supplements that I need to sustain self for my weight, height and skeletal frame. I AM reading daily high vibrational spiritual information. I AM sharpening my brain each and every day through games, puzzles and conversation. I AM acquiring the money I need to do the things that I need to do, go the places I need to go and assist the people I need to assist. I AM not a greedy person and anytime greed presents itself in my life I AM able and capable of turning away. I will turn away. So it is uttered, so it is.

9. I AM Gratitude

I AM grateful for all that I have, have had and will have. I

AM grateful for my spouse or partner if that be the case. I AM grateful for my past spouse, spouses or partners if that be the case, which causes me to be open to the new spouse or partner that awaits me. I AM grateful for my parents. I AM grateful for my children and grandchildren if that be the case. I AM grateful for my sisters or brothers and their families if that be the case. I AM grateful for my friends. I AM grateful for my employment if that be the case. I AM grateful for the ability to pay all my bills. I AM grateful for all things. I AM grateful to be a messenger of Source/God. So it is uttered, so it is.

10. I AM Peace

I AM a peaceful spiritual warrior. I AM peaceful and loving. I AM at peace with all beings, all animals, all thoughts and ideas, even if I do not agree with such. I AM able to disengage from confrontation. I AM never looking for a fight, verbally or physically. I AM, however, to always protect myself and those in my bloodline if my or their life is at risk. I AM understanding that this is totally acceptable to Source/God and the universes. So it is uttered, so it is.

11. I AM Compassion

Compassion, I AM. I AM grace, the very virtue that comes to me from Source/God. I AM knowing full well that there is not sin or hell. Therefore, I AM grace through my acceptance of my others no matter what they have done, will do, might do, say, don't say, have said. I AM compassion for I know full well that each of us on Earth behaves as we do, or have, contingent upon the information that we have received and accepted at the vibration that we may be. I AM compassion for I let all that seek hear the aforementioned words from my very being. I pity myself and others when I or they make mis-takes. I AM, however, never to beat myself up for my decisions. So it is uttered, so it is.

12. I AM Humble
I AM humus of the Earth as all creatures on planet Earth are. I AM humble for even though I know there is nothing that I can't do, I AM also knowing I need assistance from my others to accomplish those things that I am not able to do on my own. I AM humble for I understand that I have gifts and others may possess some gifts that I do not. Therefore, sometimes I must seek outside myself. So it is uttered, so it is.

13. I AM Present
I AM present for I live in the here and now. I AM in the moment for the moment is all I have. I AM in full understanding that all time is the same; the past, present and future are one. I AM present because, through understanding the moment, I AM able to use the past to live in

the present and thus positively affect the future. So it is uttered, so it is.

14. *I AM Introspective*
I AM introspective for I AM continually looking at myself. I AM introspective for each day I check myself, my thoughts, my actions. I AM introspective for I AM able to apologize to myself if I make mis-takes. I AM introspective for I AM able to apologize to others, even when my mental tells me I should or need not. I AM introspective for I am, when necessary, able to discard that which I need not anymore. I AM introspective for when I have done something to harm or hurt myself or my others, I AM able to remember that it was not of a high vibration and that it is not in my highest good to repeat such behaviors. So it is uttered, so it is.

15. *I AM Freedom of Choice*
I AM freedom of choice for I do that which I desire and wish to. I AM freedom of choice for I make my own decisions. I always have and always will. I AM freedom of choice for I fully understand that no one has ever and will ever make me do anything that I do not desire or wish to do even if, at the time, it is not in my highest good. I AM freedom of choice because by accepting such, I AM able to change, to grow, to evolve. So it is uttered, so it is.

16. I AM Hope

I AM hope for I have hope for myself, for my others, for the trees, flowers, plants, animals, mankind as a whole, the mass consciousness, our planet, for the universes. I AM hope for I believe in miracles. I AM hope for I know things can change; all things change. I AM hope for I have hope in Source/God. So it is uttered, so it is.

17. I AM Positive

I AM positive for I look at the bright side of all things. I AM positive for when I look at the glass as half-empty, I AM able to change and look at it as half-full. I AM positive for I see the God in all, even those that may not be presenting such. I AM positive for I know they can change as I have. I AM positive for I look to the positive future of myself, my others and planet Earth. So it is uttered, so it is.

18. I AM Radiant

I AM radiant for all whom see my face and hear my voice shall know that I AM assured of self. I AM always sending out a light of joy from my very being. I AM shining, glowing in all directions from my aura. So it is uttered, so it is.

19. I AM Love

I AM love. I was born in love; I will die in love. I AM love for I can be nothing else. I AM caring, giving, protective, honest, true, stable, grounded, centered, driving, and determined. I AM in the image of Source/God which is love. Therefore, so Love I AM. So it is uttered, so it is.

20. *I AM Never Alone*

I AM never alone for Source/God is with me, in me, through me, under me, over me, and all around me. I AM and have never been disconnected from Source/God. I AM connected to the highest vibration of all the Angels, Masters, Teachers, and Healers of past, present and future. I AM connected to all stars, galaxies and universes. I AM here. I AM there. I AM Everywhere and yet Nowhere, Now Here. I AM that which I AM. I can be nothing else. So it is uttered, so it is.

Let the Reader Read. Let the Hearer Hear! These are and shall always be the Discourses of I AM for mankind for your home, your planet, your Earth. Adhere to them and you and your world will change. Shout them to US, to self and others. Fore, they are the Keys to Ascension. You are on the path to Ascension—Continue. We Love You, Remember!

More Useful Decrees

I AM beautiful! I AM beautiful! I AM beautiful! And I AM ready for a wonderful day! I AM ready to give all that I can give and receive all that I can.

Mighty I AM Presence, do everything for me and

through me perfectly. Remove all doubt from me. Help me to speak only the purest Truth in everything I say. Keep me humble in every way, positive to the world, and forever in the service of the Divine. And so it is uttered, so it is done.

I AM protected always, at all times, from all low-vibration entities and any negative energy directed towards me and the Light for which I stand. And so it is uttered, so it is done.

I AM refreshed, re-energized, renewed, rejuvenated, and healed in the healing power and the Light of the Christ every day in every way and at all times. And so it is uttered, so it is done.

I AM my Perfect Body. I AM Eternal Youth and Beauty. I AM an instrument of peace. And so it is uttered, so it is done.

I AM a perfect expression of perfect love here and now. I AM patient, kind, understanding, and respectful towards all those who do not understand or are unwilling to accept my beliefs. And so it is uttered, so it is done.

I AM making a positive difference in the lives of humanity. I AM helping humanity to awaken and expand their minds in a positive, loving way. And so it is uttered, so it is done.

I AM releasing NOW, with ease and grace, all that no longer serves me and my path so that I may fulfill my life's purpose here on Earth. And so it is uttered, so it is done.

Faith

Miracles are the norm for those with faith.
~ Source/God through Elliott Eli Jackson

A strong faith can overcome any fear. Faith is the substance of things hoped for and the evidence of things not yet seen. Faith is knowing; faith is believing. Faith is confidence in someone or something. Faith is trust in God and in the process of life. Faith does not question.

Faith allows us to grow. Faith is trusting in the outcome, no matter what it might be. Faith is comforting when facing serious problems or stressful situations. Faith is the evidence of things not seen. Faith is never giving up or losing sight of a goal.

Faith is to know we will always have what we need. Faith is allowing life to unfold. Faith is victory. Faith is freedom. Faith is a virtue.

Through Faith, miracles happen!

Ho'oponopono

Ihaleakala Hew Len, Ph.D., was a master teacher who cured every patient in the criminally insane ward of a Hawaii State Hospital without ever seeing a single patient. He used an ancient Hawaiian practice known as Ho'oponopono.

Everyone in our life is an aspect of us. We all play roles

for each other. For example, an addict you know may be reflecting what you may have been in the past (past lives included). When you work to heal this aspect of yourself, you help heal the addict.

Healing takes place through the repetition of four simple statements:

I'm sorry.

Please forgive me.

Thank you.

I love you.

Close your eyes. Picture the person that is a reflection of you in your mind, and then recite these four simple statements with sincerity. The more you recite them, the sooner the healing can take place.

Ho'opopono heals through loving one's self. This powerful healing process can "clear your mind of unconscious blocks to help you get what you truly want from life. It clears beliefs, thoughts, and memories from past lives that hold you back in your current life."

In addition, Dr. Len suggests filling a blue glass bottle with the purest water you can find. Set the bottle in the sunlight (preferably outside) for 10 to 60 minutes, or up to 12 hours for a stronger effect. This will charge the water with a healing blue light. If no sun is available, use incandescent lighting. Do not use LED or fluorescent lighting. Set your intention for the "blue water" to remove recurring memories or behavior patterns playing in the background, freeing you from their effects. [14]

Give it the test of time. Based on my own personal experience, Ho'oponopono really does work.

How to Recognize True Messengers

With the thinning of the veil, more and more people are able to channel information today, but it is important to note not all of the information channeled comes from high-vibrational beings (even if the person channeling claims it does). There are tricksters in the spirit realm, and if the person channeling the information is not of a high vibration, neither is their information.

"Be on guard against false prophets, who come to you in sheep's clothing but underneath are wolves on the prowl. You will know them by their deeds." (Matthew 7: 15-16)[15]

Discernment must be used to recognize the characteristics of a true messenger. To recognize a true messenger of the Divine as stated in *Man—His Origin, History and Destiny:*[16]

- Dictations are clear and concise, containing much substance, detail, and hard facts. Dictations that deal in generalities are not or a true messenger. Messages do not contain any "fluff" or amount of "feel good."
- A true messenger focuses how to gain personal

ascension and how to bring in the next Golden Age. A true messenger will teach self-mastery.
- Is the motive of the channel to serve the Light or for personal and/or monetary gain? The key personality trait of a true messenger is true humility. Spiritual pride brought down Atlantis and Lemuria. If the channeled information feeds the ego of the channel even one crumb, it is not from the Divine. Beloved Master Kuthumi taught: "That which, even most subtly, stimulates the lower bodies and the soul to personal aggrandizement and inflation of the separate ego, is not of God."[17]
- A true messenger does not charge for channeled information. "Freely have you received; freely shall you give."[18] A reasonable fee is allowed to be charged for expenses for printing of books and brochures, travel for speaking engagements, etc. If someone charges a large amount for channeled information, that person is not of a high vibration. Greed has entered into the equation, and there is no place for greed when doing Lightwork.
- A true messenger does not assume any titles such as Master, Goddess, Guru, or Vicar of Christ. It is egoic; the messenger is not who he/she claims to be.

- In order to maintain a high vibration, the messenger needs to refrain from eating meat whenever possible. Eating meat can dull the senses.
- A true messenger must have a high state of spiritual development and training (current or past lives). All channeled information must be available for all of mankind. The student must use discernment and test to make sure the information is of a high vibration. Information should not be accepted on faith alone. Question, question, question everything, again and again. Master Kuthumi: "Many false mediators have come, but you can always test their reality in this manner: If their teaching turns the outer self to the individual I AM Presence, that mediator comes from God. If such a teacher makes the individual dependent on his/her personal identity and keeps the aspirant looking to him or her for instruction and guidance, rather than his own divine source, then such a one is not a true mediator. To misrepresent the truth is not the will of God."[19]
- A true messenger does not make students dependent on him/her. If the information does not guide the student to look at him or herself or to go within for answers, the messenger is not of a

high vibration. If the messenger teaches that one can become an angel, he or she is not of a high vibration. A spirit in human form can never be an angel.
- A true messenger will ask their students to raise their own vibration through decrees. A true messenger will ask their students to develop a healthy, strong physical body, the temple of the living God.
- Masters never threaten or use force. "A true messenger is always in full control of his faculties at all times. He can stop hearing the messages at will. There is no shaking of the physical form or "possession" that takes place when a channel is under the control of an entity."[20]
- A true channel knows he/she is responsible (karma) for any misrepresentation to the student. A true messenger gives credit where credit is due.
- A true messenger does not predict the date of a cataclysm or a great shift in mankind. There is no time on the Other Side. Time was created by man, for man.
- A true messenger can be recognized by the fruits of their labor. Their many accomplishments and miracles will be the result of their work.

"Adhering to the truth means change, change in attitude and behavior, even change in friends and your way of life. Most students resist change. The Masters said that the Goddess of Truth is not very popular with mankind. However, the Goddess of Love and Mercy are very popular. "[21] The Truth shall set you free.

When the student is ready, the teacher will come. There is no magic fairy wand that will take you into the New Age or keep you from being responsible for what you created.

Do not rely on just one channel or one book, for there is much information already published. You do not need to go from channel to channel to discover the latest truths.

Listen to Your Inner Guidance

It is important to know the difference between that which is your inner guidance and that which is not. Information is received in the same way—thought.

Your Ego

Ego is "Edging God Out." It is self-centered instead of other-centered. It works for the good of self, not for the good of all. It will either inflate you or deflate you, depending on how you feel and what you want to hear at the moment. Examples:

"Don't go out with that loser, or he'll ruin your reputation."

"That piece of apple pie is going straight to her thighs!"

Logic

Logic is the mental voice that uses past experience, statistics, probability, and reason to communicate with you. It is based on knowledge and facts. You draw on logic from your own and others' experiences. Examples:

"The last time you tried doing that you broke your ankle. Chances are you'll probably hurt it again."

"There's a traffic jam ahead. Reroute so you will get you there faster."

Spirit Guides

Your spirit guides know the bigger picture, while your ego lives in the moment. Their job is to keep you on track with your life plan. This sometimes means you may not like what they have to say. For instance, they might see the best way to teach you to value money is through bankruptcy. Examples:

"You'd be wise to accept the job in Los Angeles. It's what you've been waiting for your whole life."

"You know in your heart that he's not right for you."

Low Vibrations

Low vibrations work to keep you spirit down and take you off your spiritual path. They whisper negative thoughts in your ear that feed upon stored traumas and fears. They keep you in a state of fear. They incite prejudices and racism.

They gain control over you through addiction. They can even try to get you to hurt or kill another. You believe what they have to say. You feel anxious and depressed because your vibration is low. Examples:

"Nobody loves you."

"You don't need to exercise today. So what if you miss a day! It won't hurt you."

"He doesn't love you so you might as well cheat on him."

Know your energy! Know when lower vibration entities are on you. Don't let them play you. Work to release them. Work to raise your vibration. Be the power plant so they will stay away.

Manifestation

Use the power of creative visualization to create positive changes in your life. It can help to achieve your goals and overcome limitations, and it can promote success in every aspect of your life.

Ten proven steps to manifest your desires include:[22]

1. **Motive:** What is the purpose of your desire? Is it for the very best and highest good for all concerned?
2. **Meditate:** Visualize a clear picture of the desired result and feel how happy you will be when it happens. Do not focus on how you will achieve this or you limit the Divine as to the possibilities of how it will take place. Hold that vision.

3. **Walk away:** Give yourself time to decide if this is what you really want. Revise your visualization, if necessary. Once you content with your desired visualization, do not make any changes. Create a vision board to help manifest your desire, using markers and magazine pictures.
4. **Decree:** "I AM the full manifestation of my heart's desire, and I ask my desire to be fulfilled." Say it out loud with meaning. Feel it in your heart. When you say the words, "I AM," you are calling on God, the Great I Am, to help bring your heart's desire into manifestation. Don't let obstacles deter you. Shift negative thoughts into positive thoughts. BELIEVE, knowing that all things are possible with God.
5. **Ask for help:** Ask the Source/God and all of the Divine to protect your vision and to energize it with their own feeling, mastery, and confidence. Give gratitude in advance for your desire already taking place. In return for their assistance, be in service in some way to help increase the Light of the world.
6. **Repeat:** Repeat this every day, preferably in the morning when your mind is clear.
7. **Maintain:** Maintain a sense of calm until your manifestation occurs.

8. **Do not share your vision with anyone:** Other people's negative thoughts ("They can't do it; that's impossible!") can affect the outcome. They may also be a reflection of your own self-doubt.
9. **Repeat:** Repeat your decree and give gratitude for the help received every day until the manifestation occurs. Never give up!
10. **Journal:** Journal your experience. Journaling adds to the momentum needed to achieve success.

Prayer and Meditation

> *"Silence is essential. We need silence, just as much as we need air, just as much as plants need light. If our minds are crowded with words and thoughts, there is no space for us."* ~ Thich Nhat Hanh

Prayer is speaking to God, and meditation is listening to God.

Prayer and meditation have a profound effect on our well-being. People who pray and meditate daily have lower stress levels, age less and live longer, and maintain a state of calm. They are better prepared to handle the trials and tribulations of life.

Ten minutes a day is better than one hour a week; 30 minutes a day is preferred. Make it a regular habit. Talk to

God out loud; talk about anything and everything—what you like, what you don't like, what you want out of life. Exercise patience. Recognize when your prayer has been answered; give gratitude. Give gratitude for unanswered prayers. Unanswered prayers are quite often prayers that have been answered.

A regular practice of prayer and meditation will help you progress on your spiritual journey. It is a way to open and expand your mind, to stay in touch with your inner self, and to keep you from getting caught up in worldly ways; it will keep darkness away.

Through prayer and meditation you learn patience, releasing, hope, faith, trust, love, and true happiness. Your connection to God and all of the Divine strengthens each time you pray and meditate. You know that you are never really alone. You know that you are loved.

How to Pray

Most people pray over and over for the same thing. These repetitive prayers demonstrate a lack of faith in the person reciting the prayer.

The correct way to pray is to state your request, and then give gratitude in advance for what you would like. This shows you have faith and trust your request will be answered.

An analogy: A mother goes into the grocery store with her child. The child asks the mother for a candy bar, and the mother tells the child he can have one when she checks out if he is good while she shops.

The child goes through the store, whining and complaining, "Mommy, I want my candy bar. Mommy, I want it now. Mommy, when can I have my candy bar? Mommy, why can't I have it? I want it NOW, Mommy!" If you were the child's mother, wouldn't you want to take the child out of the store and go home?

A trusting child would go through the store saying, "Thank you for the candy bar I'm going to get, Mommy. I really appreciate it. It's going to taste really good. I'm going to love it. Thank you, Mommy. You're the best!" If you were the child's mother, wouldn't you want to hurry up shopping to give this child three candy bars?

Praying over and over for the same thing shows a lack faith. Instead pray for what you want, and then give gratitude in advance for what will take place, it shows you have faith. Gratitude is the highest form of prayer there is.

How to Meditate

Meditation begins when thinking ends. Mastering the technique of meditation takes much practice; it takes commitment. Meditation and reaching deeper spiritual states must be experienced. The amount of effort you put into your practice will determine the outcome.

Meditation has great health benefits. It can strengthen the immune system and lower blood pressure as the heart beats more slowly. Meditation helps foster a healthy mind to release negative mental states—fear, worry, and anger—and it can replace these emotions with positive attitudes. It can help to release stress, anxiety, and depression. It can help you to feel more relaxed, more peaceful, and more cheerful. Meditation can give you the ability to be more centered and more in control of yourself. As you can see, it can help to improve all areas of your life.

There are three stages to meditation: relax the body and mind, concentrate on the breath or an object, and expand your sense of being to realize you are in unity with all of creation.

Meditate daily with your eyes open for 10 minutes to align your bodies and to be at peace. Meditate once a week for 30 to 60 minutes with your eyes closed for a deeper connection to God.

The best time to meditate is in the morning when you first wake up, before eating. Set aside a place that is only used for meditation if you can to create a meditative mood and raise the vibration of the room. You can also mediate in nature.

A good way to meditate is to sit on a straight-backed chair. Sit slightly away from the back of the chair, keeping your spine erect (especially the lower spine) to avoid unnecessary pressure, and place your palms upright at the junction of the thighs and hips. Bring your shoulders back a bit to keep from slumping.

Begin and end your meditation with a prayer. Meditation helps align all your bodies so synchronicity can take place in your life. When energy is flowing through you, everything flows in life.

Answers to your prayers may show up in the words of a song, the words of another person, a sign on a truck or building, or in other ways. Be open to what life is showing you.

To Meditate with Your Eyes Open

Begin by taking three or four deep, cleansing breaths, in through the nose and out through the mouth. Relax your body, then focus on something inside or outside the room that moves. This can be a flag or tree blowing, the flicker of a candle flame, or a rotating ceiling fan. The movement of the object will help move the thoughts from your mind. Spend 10 minutes in meditation and your day will flow smoothly. You will sleep better, and you will be more at peace throughout the day.

Raising Your Vibration

Prayer and meditation, music and beauty are tools typically used to raise your vibration, but then reality settles in and our vibration goes right back to where it once was. To raise your vibration more permanently, release the many traumas and fears held in your energy field.

Our energy field holds all of our memories, fears, and traumas from current and past lives. Imagine this energy field dotted with tiny pixels, black or white in color. Black pixels represent traumas and fears, while white pixels represent pleasant, happier times and love. From a distance, our energy field looks gray. The darker the gray, the more fearful we are. The lighter the gray, the more of love we become.

Most of us have energy fields that are 51 percent or more gray. In other words, we have more fears and traumas stored than we could ever imagine! Fear is the result of a trauma. Heal the trauma that created the fear, and then work to overcome the fear.

Heal the past to heal the present. The more healing that takes place, the softer, more peaceful, and more loving we become.

Relationships

People come and go in our life. Some were only meant to be in our life for a short period of time. They provide some purpose, but soon fade away.

Some people are amazing in the beginning, but they take more than they are willing to give. They offer little help and support, especially during challenging times, and eventually fade away.

And then there are people who stay with you for a long time, especially when things get tough. We depend on them through good times and bad. And with time, even these people fade away. Sometimes they come back, and the relationship gets stronger.

People come and go in our life just as we come and go in the lives of others. For every ending, there is a new beginning. We grow together and we grow apart. This is the cycle of life.

There are times when we are left standing, feeling alone, like nobody cares. And then along comes someone else who is just like us, and we're on to a new beginning. We were never meant to be alone. If we are, it is by choice (consciously or unconsciously).

As long as we are in a relationship, we are getting something out of it, such as love, support, attention, or money. When the relationship is no longer fed, one person departs, leaving the other to feel abandoned and betrayed because we didn't see it coming. The signs are always there if you look.

Not everyone you lose in life is a loss. You shared gifts and received blessings. Move on. They were not meant to be permanent.

Don't let anyone hold you back. Allow yourself to grow. Don't be held back by someone who isn't ready to grow.

It is through the challenging times that relationships grow stronger or fall apart. A true friend can't make our problems disappear, but they won't disappear when times get tough. Recognize true friends as you open yourself up to deeper, more meaningful relationships.

Treasure the friends who care, and release those who no longer serve you. Accept the roles we play for each other. Look for the blessing in every relationship.

Release Letters

You can't change what happened, but you can change how you feel about what happened. Releasing someone heals all wounds. True release comes from the heart. It frees the soul to move on. Words are easily spoken, but not always meant.

Apologize for whatever you may have contributed to the situation, intentionally or unintentionally, and release whomever may have hurt you. And don't forget to apologize to yourself for your lack of understanding. If you are the victim, you were probably the perpetrator at some point in time. You may be getting back something you once gave out (karma).

Apologize for not accepting others for who they are, and release yourself for not accepting yourself for who you are.

Many people pray to God for forgiveness because it is much easier to ask God than to face the person we hurt. Apologize to the person hurt. You do not need God's forgiveness for, in Truth, you have never done anything wrong—only experienced! God knows both parties are learning lessons through their experiences. It is important to apologize to the person you hurt. Accept responsibility for your mistake and work to heal the situation. If the person you need to apologize to has crossed over, write a release letter to them. It will benefit both of you.

Releasing is a requirement if true and lasting change is desired.

Release Letter to Someone Else

Do this for others first, then for the self—you will be amazed at how powerful this letter really is!

Write a letter to whomever you need to release or to whom you must apologize; be sincere. If the letter is not written from the heart, nothing will change. Do not write the letter if you still hold a grudge against someone. Your intention must be pure.

This is a wonderful tool to release old emotions (current and past lives). Write anything you would like to say. You can even swear. The important thing is to get "stuck" negative thoughts and emotions out so you can be at peace. For example, you can say: "You hurt me when…" "Why did you do that? What were you trying to prove?" "How could you do that to me? You really hurt me." "That was dumb! What were you thinking?!"

Release this person who has hurt you, intentionally or unintentionally, all the way back to the root where the problem began (this is very important). Heal the past to heal the present. When looking at the weed on top of the ground (current life), you do not see the roots hidden beneath the ground (past lives).

Apologize for anything you may have done to hurt this person, intentionally or unintentionally, in your many lifetimes together (current and past). Most likely, you both have contributed to the problem in one lifetime or another, and that is why you are together now. Unresolved issues keep us tied together throughout eternity until they are resolved.

Send love to this person—all the way back to the root life. At the end of the letter, include this statement:

"I love you very much, and I release you. I apologize for not accepting you exactly as you are."

Take your letter to a place that is sacred to you and to God, and then read it out loud.

Tear the letter up, then burn it. Make sure every last piece of paper is burnt (symbolic of purification). You don't want to leave anything behind.

Now take the ashes outside and say:

"Dear God, this has been a burden I no longer wish to carry. Please resolve it for me in the Divine White Light of the Holy Spirit. Gratitude."

Toss the ashes into the wind.

Visualize an etheric cord that binds the two of you together by removing it from you first, then the other person. This cord can usually be found at the solar plexus, although it can be anywhere. Place the cord into the Platinum Flame. You will feel different!

Release Letter to Yourself
Write a letter to yourself, writing from the heart. This is a wonderful tool to release old stuck emotions (current and past lives). Write anything you would like to say to yourself. You can even swear, if so desired. The important thing is to get "stuck" negative thoughts and emotions out so you can be at peace. When you have peace within, there is peace in your world.

In the letter, you can say anything you want. For example, you can ask yourself: "Why did you say/do that?" "That was dumb! What were you thinking?!" "Why did you make that decision about that job?" "Why do you keep falling into the same old trap?"

Be sure to address any fears you may have that you are ready to release, anything you don't like about yourself, and any problems you may have with someone else (they are a mirror back to you).

Release yourself for whatever you feel you may have done wrong (for being too judgmental or critical of yourself, for doubting yourself, for not loving yourself, etc.).

Release yourself for not accepting you for who you really are—a work in progress. (We strive for perfection, but we are not there yet!)

And be sure to send love to yourself.

At the end of the letter, include this statement:

"I love you very much, and I release you. I apologize for not accepting you exactly as you are."

Take your letter to a place that is sacred to you and to God, and then read it out loud.

Tear the letter up, then burn it. Make sure every last piece of paper is burnt (symbolic of purification). You don't want to leave anything behind.

Then look in the mirror into your eyes (the eyes are the entrance way to the soul) and say:

"I release you, and I love you very much."

Now take the ashes outside and say:

"Dear God, this has been a burden I no longer wish to carry. Please resolve it for me in the Divine White Light of the Holy Spirit. Gratitude."

Toss the ashes into the wind. You will feel different!

Trust and Surrender

Just when you think nothing is going to happen, something will happen. So don't give up!
~ Source/God through Elliott Eli Jackson

We have been learning life lessons through experience. Trust and surrender are required in order to release fear. Trust in the process of life, and surrender to the outcome. Let go and let God!

When you surrender yourself to God, the universe will provide all the situations and opportunities needed to balance all your issues and bring about healing. When you surrender to the process with absolute faith and trust, without judgment or fear, you can get through any situation with ease and grace.

Old negative behavioral patterns and belief systems that block love must be released. When we surrender to God, it will no longer matter what other people think of us. We will begin to follow our own truth and listen to our own heart.

The first step is the hardest and most overwhelming. As Lao-Tzu taught, the journey of a thousand miles begins with the first step. The first step is always the hardest. Trust that once you have taken the first step, the rest will be much easier. The more you practice this, the more you will succeed.

Endnotes

1. http://www.thebestofrawfood.com/ph-test-strips.html
2. https://www.healthline.com/health/healthy-sleep/foods-that-could-boost-your-serotonin
3. https://blog.thatcleanlife.com/5-foods-that-fight-symptoms-of-depression/
4. https://universityhealthnews.com/daily/depression/8-natural-dopamine-boosters-to-overcome-depression/
5. *Modern Essentials*, @ 2016 Aroma Tools™. All rights reserved.
6. http://www.ams.usda.gov/AMSv1.0/ams.fetchTemplateData.do?template=TemplateN&leftNav=NationalOrganicProgram&page=NOPGoingOrganic&description=Going%2520Organic
7. http://www.aarp.org/food/healthy-eating/info-04-2012/real-organic-food.html
8. http://www.natural-health-well.com/how-do-essential-oils-work
9. http://www.cdc.gov/healthyweight/physical_activity/index.html
10. *The Sapiential Discourses: Universal Wisdom*, by All There Is Was and Ever Shall Be through Elliott Eli Jackson, © 2012 Independently published, All rights reserved.
11. https://sciencing.com/what-functions-umbilical-cord-4672809.html
12. *The Ascension Flame of Purification and Immortality* by Aurelia Louise Jones, © 2017 by Aurelia Louise Jones, Mt. Shasta Light Publishing, Mount Shasta, CA.

13 *The Sapiential Discourses: Universal Wisdom Book* III, by All There Is Was and Ever Shall Be through Elliott Eli Jackson, © 2017 Independently published, All rights reserved.
14 https://bluebottlelove.com/hew-len-hooponopono/
15 *The New American Bible,* © 1971 Catholic Publishers, Inc., All rights reserved.
16 *Man—His Origin, History and Destiny,* © 1984 Ascended Master Teaching Foundation, Mount Shasta, CA. All rights reserved.
17 *Man—His Origin, History and Destiny,* © 1984 Ascended Master Teaching Foundation, Mount Shasta, CA. All rights reserved.
18 Ibid.
19 Ibid.
20 Ibid.
21 Ibid.
22 *The Law of Precipitation: How to Successfully Meet Life's Daily Needs* by Werner Schroeder, © 2000 Ascended Master Teaching Foundation, Mount Shasta, CA.

White Dove Circle of Light and Love

is a unique, one-of-a-kind wellness center where one can find true healing for the mind, body, and spirit.

Everyone has his or her own unique and different issues to heal, and because our issues differ, no two people heal in the same way.

White Dove Circle is a leader in the holistic field offering a wide variety of services and products to heal naturally.

Step into our beautiful wellness center and you immediately feel a sense of calm; a sense of peace. You know that where you are…is where you're supposed to be!

Come share your heart with us!

White Dove Circle of Light and Love
205 East Street
Springboro, OH 45066
937.806.3231
info@whitedovecircle.com
whitedovecircle.org

We are the Community of White Dove

SERVICE to Creator/God, to all of the Divine, and to all of our fellow man through:

    Compassion—understanding what others are going through, sharing our love with them

    Mercy—lending a helping hand to those who need it the most

    Joy—finding joy in everyone and everything in life; helping others find their joy

PEACE—inner and outer peace through:

    Humility—recognizing we are all one and that no one is better than another

    Purity—in our thoughts, words, actions, and deeds; in the way we live our life

    Devotion—having a strong connection with Creator/God and all of the Divine through prayer and meditation

RELEASING—of self and others through:

    Faith—in Creator/God and all of the Divine, knowing everything happens for a reason and a purpose

    Hope—for a better relationship with one's self and with others, doing our part to create a better world

    Trust—that through releasing we will find a much deeper love—unconditional love

TRUTH—the purest truth there is, standing strong in this truth through:

> **Sincerity**—in all we say and all we do, always working from a place of love
>
> **Loyalty**—to Creator/God and all of the Divine, to one's self (to thine own self be true)
>
> **Courage**—to speak our truth and to stand in our truth even when others do not understand

LIGHT AND LOVE—the foundation on which we are built

> **Loving** with all our hearts and all our souls, all of life and all of creation
>
> **Spreading** our light wherever we go to light the way for others to follow
>
> **Sharing** the Wisdom of the Masters with those who seek the Truth

Come share your heart with us!

www.ingramcontent.com/pod-product-compliance
Lightning Source LLC
Chambersburg PA
CBHW071708040426
42446CB00011B/1967